Europe and Iran

Perspectives on
Non-proliferation

G000144780

Stockholm International Peace Research Institute

SIPRI is an independent international institute for research into problems of peace and conflict, especially those of arms control and disarmament. It was established in 1966 to commemorate Sweden's 150 years of unbroken peace.

The Institute is financed mainly by a grant proposed by the Swedish Government and subsequently approved by the Swedish Parliament. The staff and the Governing Board are international. The Institute also has an Advisory Committee as an international consultative body.

The Governing Board is not responsible for the views expressed in the publications of the Institute.

Governing Board
Ambassador Rolf Ekéus, Chairman (Sweden)
Sir Marrack Goulding, Vice-Chairman (United Kingdom)
Dr Alexei G. Arbatov (Russia)
Dr Willem F. van Eekelen (Netherlands)
Dr Nabil Elaraby (Egypt)
Rose E. Gottemoeller (United States)
Professor Helga Haftendorn (Germany)
Professor Ronald G. Sutherland (Canada)
The Director

Director
Alyson J. K. Bailes (United Kingdom)

sipri

Stockholm International Peace Research Institute
Signalistgatan 9, SE-169 70 Solna, Sweden
Telephone: 46 8/655 97 00
Telefax: 46 8/655 97 33
Email: sipri@sipri.org
Internet URL: http://www.sipri.org

Europe and Iran

Perspectives on Non-proliferation

SIPRI Research Report No. 21

Edited by
Shannon N. Kile

OXFORD UNIVERSITY PRESS
2005

OXFORD

UNIVERSITY PRESS

Great Clarendon Street, Oxford OX2 6DP

Oxford University Press is a department of the University of Oxford.
It furthers the University's objective of excellence in research, scholarship,
and education by publishing worldwide in

Oxford New York

Auckland Cape Town Dar es Salaam Hong Kong Karachi
Kuala Lumpur Madrid Melbourne Mexico City Nairobi
New Delhi Shanghai Taipei Toronto

With offices in

Argentina Austria Brazil Chile Czech Republic France Greece
Guatemala Hungary Italy Japan Poland Portugal Singapore
South Korea Switzerland Thailand Turkey Ukraine Vietnam

Oxford is a registered trade mark of Oxford University Press
in the UK and in certain other countries

Published in the United States
by Oxford University Press Inc., New York

© SIPRI 2005

First published 2005

All rights reserved. No part of this publication may be reproduced,
stored in a retrieval system, or transmitted, in any form or by any means,
without the prior permission in writing of SIPRI, or as expressly permitted by law,
or under terms agreed with the appropriate reprographics rights organizations.
Enquiries concerning reproduction outside the scope of the above should be sent to
SIPRI, Signalistgatan 9, SE-169 70 Solna, Sweden

You must not circulate this book in any other binding or cover
and you must impose the same condition on any acquirer

British Library Cataloguing in Publication Data
Data available

Library of Congress Cataloging in Publication Data
Data available

Typeset and originated by Stockholm International Peace Research Institute
Printed and bound in Great Britain
on acid-free paper by
Biddles Ltd, King's Lynn, Norfolk

ISBN 0-19-929087-3   978-0-19-929087-1
ISBN 0-19-929088-1   978-0-19-929088-8 (*pbk*)

Contents

Preface

The engagement of three of the largest member states of the European Union (EU), and of the official organs of the Union, with Iran over the issue of nuclear non-proliferation has been part of a larger learning process for both sides. The EU approaches it as a test case—of internationally acknowledged importance—for its own new proactive strategy on weapons of mass destruction (WMD) and for its recently formulated objectives as a strategic actor on world security issues generally. Negotiating from the other side is an Iranian elite and Iranian society that are still locked in the search for a sustainable form of governance at home, and for a place in the world that is both secure and in tune with Iranian ambitions.

On 23 May 2004 SIPRI and its Iranian partner institute, the Institute for Political and International Studies (IPIS), were enabled with generous support from the foreign ministries of Ireland and Finland to hold a round-table seminar in Tehran on 'Europe's approach to regional security'. Thirteen researchers, officials and other experts from Europe and the USA and more than 25 Iranians took part. The aim was not to dig out facts or adopt judgements on the possible military applications of Iran's civil nuclear programme, and still less to second-guess the very specific negotiations on that issue that were under way between Iran and European representatives at the time. Rather, SIPRI's initiative sought to encourage the clearest possible statement of each side's approaches and of the historical, political and conceptual depths behind them, with a view to trying to understand to what extent Iran and Europe could, in fact, understand each other on this issue—or on any other.

The present Research Report collects together work by a number of European and Iranian experts based on, and completed since, the 2004 seminar. Following the same philosophy, it juxtaposes the different contributions rather than trying to suppress or reconcile their differences (although Shannon Kile's introduction aims, in part, to provide a factual framework that should assist all readers in approaching the issue). The big picture that emerges from these materials is one of differences, or only partial overlaps, between the European and Iranian frames of reference on regional security and proliferation that go far to explain why a solution in the negotiations has been so elusive—even leaving aside the major and probably decisive complication represented by the role of the USA (and other third parties). At the same time, the authors provide much useful information on topics that are not usually linked together in this way, such as the details of the EU's new strategy-building exercise; the sequence of transactions between Iran, the International Atomic Energy Agency (IAEA) and the European states; Iran's own security and defence structures, policies and influences; and the way in which different Iranian authorities interact in the process of security policy decision making.

The cut-off date for the material is June 2005, shortly after the Iranian presidential elections.

Special thanks are due to the IPIS and to H. E. Christofer Gyllenstierna, Sweden's ambassador in Tehran, for the excellent arrangements surrounding the 2004 seminar, and to the Irish and Finnish foreign ministries for supporting the full range of activities under this project. Heidar Ali Balouji, the IPIS's resident representative at the Embassy of Iran in Sweden, has given invaluable practical support for SIPRI's exchanges with Iran as well as contributing on a personal basis to this volume. Thanks are due to Shannon Kile as editor of the Research Report and coordinator of the entire EU–Iran project; to SIPRI colleagues for their help; to all the authors represented here; and to Eve Johansson and the SIPRI Editorial and Publications Department for the editorial work. It should, however, be stressed that each contributor to this volume has the sole personal responsibility for the materials presented and for the opinions expressed.

Alyson J. K. Bailes
Director, SIPRI
August 2005

Acronyms and abbreviations

ACP	African, Caribbean and Pacific
AEOI	Atomic Energy Organization of Iran
BTWC	Biological and Toxin Weapons Convention
CFSP	Common Foreign and Security Policy
CODUN	Committee on Disarmament issues at the United Nations
CONOP	Committee on Non-Proliferation
COREPER	Committee of the Permanent Representatives to the EU
CTBT	Comprehensive Nuclear Test-Ban Treaty
CWC	Chemical Weapons Convention
E3	France, Germany and the United Kingdom
EMAA	Euro-Mediterranean Association Agreement
EU	European Union
G8	Group of Eight industrialized countries
GAERC	General Affairs and External Relations Council
HCOC	Hague Code of Conduct against Ballistic Missile Proliferation
HEU	Highly enriched uranium
IAEA	International Atomic Energy Agency
IRGC	Islamic Revolutionary Guards Corps
LEU	Low-enriched uranium
MKO	Mujahedin Khalgh Organization
MP	Member of Parliament
MWe	Megawatts-electric
NATO	North Atlantic Treaty Organization
NPT	Non-Proliferation Treaty
NNWS	Non-nuclear weapon state
NSG	Nuclear Suppliers Group
PSC	Political and Security Committee
SCCAF	Supreme Command Council of the Armed Forces
SNSC	Supreme National Security Council
TCA	Trade and Co-operation Agreement
UAE	United Arab Emirates
UF_6	Uranium hexafluoride
UK	United Kingdom
UN	United Nations
UNMOVIC	UN Monitoring, Verification and Inspection Commission
WMD	Weapons of mass destruction
WMDFZ	Weapons of mass destruction-free zone
WTO	World Trade Organization

1. The controversy over Iran's nuclear programme*

Shannon N. Kile

I. Introduction

This research report is set against the background of the international controversy over the scope and nature of Iran's nuclear programme and Iran's compliance with its comprehensive safeguards agreement with the International Atomic Energy Agency (IAEA). The controversy has moved to the forefront of the international debate about the future of the nuclear non-proliferation regime and its principal legal foundation, the 1968 Treaty on the Non-Proliferation of Nuclear Weapons (Non-Proliferation Treaty, NPT). It has centred on revelations by the IAEA that Iran failed over a period of 18 years to declare important nuclear activities, in contravention of its NPT-mandated full-scope safeguards agreement with the agency.[1] Iran insists that its nuclear programme is aimed solely at producing electricity and that any safeguards violations were inadvertent. In Europe and the USA, however, there is concern that Iran is attempting to put into place, under the cover of a nuclear energy programme, the fuel-cycle facilities needed to produce fissile material—plutonium and highly enriched uranium (HEU)—for a secret nuclear weapon programme.

The stakes are high: the way in which the nuclear controversy is resolved will have a lasting impact on the viability of the NPT, which is facing a series of unprecedented internal and external challenges. The controversy has highlighted a number of shortcomings in the

---

[1] Iran acceded to the NPT on 2 Feb. 1970. Its full-scope safeguards agreement with the IAEA (INFCIRC/214) entered into force on 15 May 1974. The text of the agreement is available at URL <http://www.iaea.org/Publications/Documents/Infcircs/Others/infcirc214.pdf>.

* This chapter is partly based on material previously published by the author: Kile, S. N., 'Nuclear arms control, non-proliferation and ballistic missile defence', *SIPRI Yearbook 2003: Armaments, Disarmament and International Security* (Oxford University Press: Oxford, 2003), pp. 596–98; 'Nuclear arms control and non-proliferation', *SIPRI Yearbook 2004: Armaments, Disarmament and International Security* (Oxford University Press: Oxford, 2004), pp. 604–12; and 'Nuclear arms control and non-proliferation', *SIPRI Yearbook 2005: Armaments, Disarmament and International Security* (Oxford: Oxford University Press, 2005).

nuclear safeguards system administered by the IAEA as well as important normative tensions within the NPT. For the European Union (EU), the Iranian nuclear issue has become an important test case of its Strategy Against the Proliferation of Weapons of Mass Destruction, adopted in 2003.

This chapter provides descriptive account of the origins and development of the Iranian nuclear controversy as a factual framework for the chapters that follow in this volume. It begins with an overview of Iran's nuclear programme and of the IAEA's findings which have raised questions about the nature of that programme. It then examines the negotiations between Iran and the three EU member states France, Germany and the United Kingdom—the 'E3'—that have taken the lead in attempting to resolve the controversy, and concludes with a brief assessment of the implications of the controversy for the non-proliferation regime.

II. Overview of Iran's nuclear programme

Iran has a long-standing interest in nuclear technology. In the 1970s, during the reign of Shah Mohammed Reza Pahlavi, Iran had plans for a nuclear power programme designed to generate 23 000 megawatts-electric (MWe) of electricity.[2] The programme relied on extensive foreign assistance, especially from the United States, France and Germany. Following the 1979 Islamic Revolution, the programme came to a standstill. However, by the mid-1980s Iran was making efforts to revitalize its science and technology base, including its civilian nuclear energy programme. Iran sent numerous students abroad for nuclear training. It also signed long-term cooperation agreements with Pakistan (in 1987) and China (in 1990) to train nuclear personnel and provide technical assistance.[3] Pakistan and China later abandoned the agreements because of US pressure.

In 1995 Iran signed an $800 million deal with Russia's Ministry of Atomic Energy (Minatom) to complete a light-water power reactor, started by the German company Siemens in the 1970s, near the town

---

[2] Ghannadi-Maragheh, G., 'Atomic Energy Organization of Iran', Paper presented at the World Nuclear Association Annual Symposium 2002, World Nuclear Association, 4–6 Sep. 2002, URL <http://www.world-nuclear.org/sym/2002/ghannadi.htm>.

[3] Nuclear Threat Initiative (NTI), 'Iran: Nuclear overview', updated Feb. 2005, URL <http://www.nti.org/e_research/profiles/Iran/1819_1822.html>.

of Bushehr on the Persian Gulf.[4] The US Government sought to prevent the deal from going ahead, arguing that it might allow Iran to obtain plutonium from the spent fuel;[5] Iranian officials insisted that the Bushehr project fell entirely within the provisions of Article IV of the NPT.[6] They also noted that Russia had made its agreement to supply fuel for the reactor conditional on Iran agreeing to return all spent fuel to Russia. After a lengthy disagreement over financial and technical arrangements, Iran and Russia signed a fuel supply deal on 27 February 2005. This paved the way for the start-up of the Bushehr reactor in 2006.[7]

In 2002, Iran announced plans to construct, over the next 20 years, nuclear power plants with a total capacity of 6000 MWe (in addition to the Bushehr plant) as part of its long-term energy policy to make up for the expected depletion of its extensive fossil fuel reserves.[8] In February 2003, then President Mohammad Khatami announced that Iran planned to develop a complete nuclear fuel cycle, from mining and processing uranium ore for use in nuclear power reactors to reprocessing spent fuel and storing waste.[9] Outside experts argued that the plan made little economic sense in the light of the global surpluses of plutonium and enriched uranium. Iranian officials

[4] Albright, D., Berkhout, F. and Walker, W. (SIPRI), *Plutonium and Highly Enriched Uranium 1996: World Inventories, Capabilities and Policies* (Oxford University Press: Oxford, 1997), pp. 354–56. Russia is constructing a 1000-MWe light-water reactor for the Bushehr Nuclear Power Plant that is based on its VVER-1000 reactor.

[5] US Central Intelligence Agency, 'Unclassified report to Congress on the acquisition of technology relating to weapons of mass destruction and advanced conventional munitions, 1 July through 31 December 2000', URL <http://www.cia.gov/cia/reports/721_reports/july_dec2000.htm#3>. There was also concern in the USA that the project would allow Iran to maintain wide-ranging contacts with Russian nuclear entities and to engage in more sensitive forms of cooperation with direct applicability to a nuclear weapon programme.

[6] According to Article IV of the NPT, all Parties have an 'inalienable right' to carry out research and produce and use nuclear energy 'for peaceful purposes without discrimination'. Article IV also mandates that 'Parties to the Treaty in a position to do so' shall cooperate in contributing to the development of nuclear energy for peaceful purposes. For the full text of the NPT see URL <http://www.iaea.org/Publications/Documents/Treaties/npt.html>.

[7] Mehr News Agency, 'Iran, Russia sign deal on nuclear fuel delivery', *Tehran Times*, 28 Feb. 2005, pp. 1, 15; and Kerr, P., 'Iran, Russia reach nuclear agreement', *Arms Control Today*, vol. 35, no. 3 (Apr. 2005), URL <http://www.armscontrol.org/act/2005_04/Bushehr.asp>.

[8] Statement by H. E. Reza Aghazadeh, President of the Atomic Energy Organization of Iran, at the 46th General Conference of the International Atomic Energy Agency, Vienna, 16 Sep. 2002, URL <http://www.iaea.org/About/Policy/GC/GC46/iran.pdf>.

[9] Albright, D., 'Iran at a nuclear crossroads', Institute for Science and International Security (ISIS), Issues Brief, 20 Feb. 2003, URL <http://www.isis-online.org/publications/iran/crossroads.html>.

emphasized that the goal was to achieve self-sufficiency in fuel manufacture, thereby obviating the need for foreign suppliers who had proved to be unreliable in the past. The desire to achieve independence from outside assistance has been a leitmotif running through Iran's justifications for pursuing sensitive nuclear fuel-cycle technologies.

III. Iran and nuclear proliferation concerns

The controversy over Iran's nuclear programme arose after evidence began to emerge in the autumn of 2002 that the Atomic Energy Organization of Iran (AEOI) was building two previously undeclared nuclear fuel facilities south of Tehran.[10] In February 2003, IAEA Director General Mohamed ElBaradei travelled to Tehran for talks with Khatami and other senior Iranian officials. During the visit, the AEOI confirmed that a heavy-water production plant, which is not subject to comprehensive safeguards, was under construction near Arak in conjunction with a planned heavy-water research reactor.[11] It also acknowledged that previously undeclared pilot- and commercial-scale gas centrifuge uranium enrichment plants were under construction at Natanz.[12] The presence in the pilot plant of an operating centrifuge cascade led IAEA experts to suspect that Iran might have already introduced nuclear material into the centrifuges in order to test them—a violation of its safeguards agreement, if it were done without first informing the agency.[13] At the end of ElBaradei's visit, Iran announced that it had agreed to amend its safeguards agreement and

[10] Albright, D. and Hinderstein, C., 'Iran building nuclear fuel cycle facilities: International transparency needed', Institute for Science and International Security (ISIS), Issues Brief, 12 Dec. 2002, URL <http://www.isis-online.org/publications/iran/iranimages.html>. The facilities appeared to be designed to withstand aerial attack, which heightened international suspicion about their true purpose.

[11] Some independent experts have expressed concern about the intended purpose of the 40-MW heavy-water reactor to be built near Arak, since such reactors are well suited for producing weapon-grade plutonium. Boureston, J. and Mahaffey, C., 'Iran's IR-40 reactor: A preliminary assessment', FirstWatch International, Nov. 2003, URL <http://www.firstwatchint.org/IR40.htm>.

[12] IAEA, 'Introductory statement by IAEA Director General Mohamed ElBaradei to the Board of Governors', Vienna, 17 Mar. 2003, URL <http://www.iaea.org/NewsCenter/Statements/2003/ebsp2003n008.shtml>; and Kerr, P., 'IAEA "taken aback" by speed of Iran's nuclear program', Arms Control Today, vol. 33, no. 3 (Apr. 2003), p. 32.

[13] Article 34(c) of Iran's safeguards agreement with the IAEA stipulates that 'nuclear material of a composition and purity suitable for fuel fabrication or being isotopically enriched, or any nuclear material produced at a later stage in the nuclear fuel cycle, is subject to all of the safeguards procedure specified in the Agreement'. IAEA (note 1).

would henceforth provide the IAEA with design information on new fuel-cycle facilities when construction was first authorized.[14]

During the spring and summer of 2003, discussions were held between Iran and the IAEA aimed at clarifying a number of safeguards-related issues. These mainly had to do with Iran's reporting of its imports of nuclear material and its declaring of the facilities and other locations where the material had been stored and processed. IAEA inspectors were allowed to take environmental samples at Natanz and several other nuclear sites in order to verify the absence of undeclared nuclear material and activities.

The cooperation between Iran and the IAEA developed fitfully. ElBaradei reported to the IAEA Board of Governors on 26 August 2003 that Iran had been slow to grant agency experts full access to certain key facilities and at times had provided them with incomplete or contradictory information.[15] This and other shortcomings led the Board to adopt, on 12 September 2003, a resolution stating that it 'was essential and urgent that Iran remedy all failures identified by the Agency' by taking the 'necessary actions by the end of October 2003'.[16] It also called on Iran to promptly sign and implement an Additional Protocol to its safeguards agreement. The resolution implicitly threatened to refer the matter to the United Nations Security Council if Iran failed to resolve all outstanding issues.

Table 1.1 summarizes Iran's nuclear infrastructure relevant to IAEA safeguards as of January 2005.

---

[14] IAEA, 'Implementation of the NPT safeguards agreement in the Islamic Republic of Iran', Report by the Director General to the IAEA Board of Governors, GOV/2003/40, 6 June 2003, p. 4, URL <http://www.iaea.org/Publications/Documents/Board/2003/gov2003-69.pdf>. Under the original terms of its safeguards agreement, Iran was not obligated to provide the IAEA with design information about a nuclear facility until 180 days before the introduction of nuclear material into the facility.

[15] IAEA, 'Implementation of the NPT safeguards agreement in the Islamic Republic of Iran', Report by the Director General to the IAEA Board of Governors, GOV/2003/63, 26 Aug. 2003, p. 10, URL <http://www.iaea.org/Publications/Documents/Board/2003/gov2003-63.pdf>.

[16] IAEA, 'Implementation of the NPT safeguards agreement in the Islamic Republic of Iran', Resolution adopted by the IAEA Board of Governors, GOV/2003/69, 12 Sep. 2003, pp. 2–3, URL <http://www.iaea.org/Publications/Documents/Board/2003/gov2003-69.pdf>. The actions to be taken by Iran included: providing a full declaration of all imported material and components relevant to the enrichment programme; granting access, including environmental sampling, to all sites requested by the Agency; resolving questions about the testing of gas centrifuges with nuclear material; and providing complete information regarding uranium conversion experiments.

Table 1.1. Iran's nuclear infrastructure relevant to IAEA safeguards, January 2005

Location	Facility[a]	Status
Arak	IR-40 research reactor[b]	40-MWth heavy water reactor; construction began in 2004[c]
Bushehr	Bushehr Nuclear Power Plant	Russian-designed 1000-MWe light water reactor (scheduled to be commissioned in 2006
Esfahan Nuclear Technology Centre (ENTC)	Research reactors/ critical assemblies[d]	Operating, acquired from China
	Fuel Fabrication Laboratory	Operating since 1985, declared to IAEA in 1993
	Fuel Manufacturing Plant	Commercial-scale plant; construction began in 2004
	Uranium Conversion Facility (UCF)	Plant for converting uranium ore into UF_6 for use in domestic enrichment programme. First process units operational 2004
Karaj	Radioactive waste storage facility[b]	Under construction, partially operating
Lashkar Ab'ad	Laser isotope separation (LIS) facility	Dismantled in May 2003. Site of uranium laser enrichment experiments using undeclared uranium metal; being converted to centrifuge enrichment R&D facility
Natanz	Pilot Fuel Enrichment Plant[b]	Operational. Pilot-scale uranium enrichment plant housing $c.$ 1000 centrifuges, activities suspended Nov. 2004
	Fuel Enrichment Plant[b]	Commercial-scale plant designed to house $c.$ 50 000 centrifuges;[e] construction suspended Nov. 2004
Tehran Nuclear Research Centre (TNRC)	Tehran Research Reactor	5-MWth research reactor; operating, acquired from the USA in 1967
	Jabr Ibn Hayan Multi-purpose Laboratories[b]	Operating. Site of undeclared experiments using nuclear material, including production of uranium metal
Tehran	Kalaye Electric Company	Dismantled in mid-2003. Housed undeclared workshop for production and testing of centrifuge parts

MWe = megawatt-electric; MWth = megawatt-thermal; UF_6 = uranium hexafluoride.

[a] In addition, Iran operates 2 uranium mines: the Saghand mine, located in Yazd; and the Gchine mine, located near Bandar Abbas. Iran also has 3 uranium milling and processing facilities: a pilot yellowcake production plant at Saghand; an industrial-scale plant at Ardakan; and a uranium production plant at Bandar Abbas.

[b] Facilities first declared by Iran to the IAEA in 2003. The nuclear waste storage facilities at Arak and at the TNRC were also first declared in 2003.

 c Some non-governmental experts have estimated that the reactor could produce 8–10 kg of plutonium annually, or enough for 1 or 2 simple nuclear weapons.

 d These include the Miniature Neutron Source Reactor (MNSR); the Light Water Subcritical Reactor (LWSR); and the Heavy Water Zero Power Reactor (HWZPR). The Graphite Sub-Critical Reactor (GSCR) has been decommissioned.

 e According to one estimate, this will provide a separative capacity sufficient to produce *c.* 500 kg of HEU annually, or enough for 25–30 nuclear weapons.

Sources: IAEA, 'Implementation of the NPT safeguards agreement in the Islamic Republic of Iran', Report by the Director General to the IAEA Board of Governors, GOV/2004/83, 15 Nov. 2004, URL <http://www.iaea.org/Publications/Documents/Board/2004/gov2004-83.pdf>; Ghannadi-Maragheh, G., 'Atomic Energy Organization of Iran', Paper presented at the World Nuclear Association Annual Symposium 2002, 4–6 Sep. 2002, URL <http://www.world-nuclear.org/sym/2002/ghannadi.htm>; and Albright, D. and Hinderstein, C., 'Iran: Player or rogue?', *Bulletin of the Atomic Scientists*, vol. 59, no. 5 (Sep./Oct. 2003), pp. 52–58.

The IAEA Board's imposition of the October 2003 deadline heightened tensions over Iran's nuclear programme. Iran warned that its willingness to accept more comprehensive nuclear inspections under the Additional Protocol depended on its receiving assurances that it could develop enrichment technology for peaceful purposes. Iranian leaders also demanded that the IAEA Board resist US pressure to refer the matter to the UN Security Council.[17] At the same time, there were signs of disagreement between the USA and some of its European allies over how best to deal with Iran's safeguards violations, with the latter rejecting US calls for a more confrontational approach.[18]

The Iranian–E3 joint declaration

On 21 October 2003, following intensive negotiations in Tehran, the E3 foreign ministers issued a joint declaration with their Iranian counterpart on the nuclear issue.[19] Iran stated in the declaration that,

[17] Barringer, F., 'Iranian envoy blames US for nation's reticence on nuclear plans', *New York Times* (Internet edn), 12 Sep. 2003, URL <http://www.nytimes.com/2003/09/12/international/middleeast/12IRAN.html>; and Dinmore, G. and Turner, M., 'Iran demands a trade-off between nuclear power goals and inspections', *Financial Times*, 29 Sep. 2003, p. 1.

[18] Daalder, I. and Levi, M., 'How to counter the Iranian threat', *Financial Times*, 24 Sep. 2003, p. 13; and Taylor, P. and Charbonneau, L., 'Defying US, 3 European nations engage Iran on nuclear program', Reuters, *Washington Post* (Internet edn), 20 Sep. 2003, URL <http://www.washingtonpost.com/>.

[19] BBC News (Internet edn), 'Iran agrees to key nuclear demands', 22 Oct. 2003, URL <http://news.bbc.co.uk/1/hi/world/middle_east/3210574.stm>.

after having received the necessary clarifications, it would sign an Additional Protocol to its safeguards agreement.[20] It also stated that, as an additional confidence-building measure, it would voluntarily suspend all enrichment and reprocessing activities. However, Iran did not specify in the declaration or in subsequent statements how long the moratorium would last or what its scope of application would be. The three European governments recognized Iran's right to pursue the peaceful use of nuclear energy in accordance with the NPT. They noted that, once Iran acted to fully resolve concerns about its nuclear programme, it 'could expect easier access to modern technology and supplies in a range of areas'.[21] It was unclear whether this meant that they would provide assistance for nuclear energy projects in Iran.

Unresolved safeguards compliance issues

While the signing of the joint declaration defused, at least temporarily, a growing crisis over Iran's nuclear activities, there remained numerous concerns about the nature and aim of those activities. On 10 November 2003, Director General ElBaradei sent a report to the IAEA Board that described a nuclear programme that was both more extensive and more advanced than previously believed, as well having been kept hidden from international scrutiny for decades.[22] It also described multiple instances of undeclared foreign assistance that had provided Iran with components, material and technical expertise used in its enrichment programme.[23] While ElBaradei concluded that there was 'no evidence' that the country's previously undeclared nuclear activities were related to a military programme, he said that 'given Iran's past pattern of concealment, it

---

[20] IAEA, 'Statement by the Iranian Government and visiting EU foreign ministers', Tehran, 21 Oct. 2003, URL <http://www.iaea.org/NewsCenter/Focus/IaeaIran/statement_iran 21102003.shtml>. The text is reproduced in appendix A.

[21] IAEA (note 20).

[22] IAEA, 'Implementation of the NPT safeguards agreement in the Islamic Republic of Iran', Report by the Director General to the IAEA Board of Governors, GOV/2003/75, 10 Nov. 2003, p. 9, URL <http://www.iaea.org/Publications/Documents/Board/2003/gov 2003-75.pdf>.

[23] Pakistan's role came under particular scrutiny, since IAEA inspectors discovered that Iran's clandestine enrichment programme used an advanced centrifuge that was identical to a Pakistani design. Broad, W., Sanger, D. and Bonner, R., 'A tale of nuclear proliferation: how Pakistani built his network', *New York Times* (Internet edn), 12 Feb. 2004, URL <http://www.nytimes.com/2004/02/12/international/asia/12NUKE.html>.

will take time before the Agency is able to conclude that Iran's nuclear programme is exclusively for peaceful purposes'.[24]

ElBaradei's report identified three outstanding issues which the agency was working with Iran to clarify.

Uranium enrichment. Iran began a gas-centrifuge uranium enrichment programme in 1985. The results of environmental samples taken by IAEA inspectors at the Natanz pilot gas-centrifuge enrichment plant in the spring of 2003 revealed particles of both low-enriched uranium (LEU) and HEU. This suggested that Iran had produced HEU—a possibility which alarmed many analysts since none of Iran's power reactors require HEU. The Iranian authorities attributed the presence of the particles to contamination originating from imported centrifuge components.[25] However, this explanation contradicted Iran's previous insistence that the programme was completely indigenous.

Iran also had been pursuing a laser-based uranium-enrichment programme since 1991. From 2002 to 2003 it conducted secret laser enrichment experiments at a pilot facility using undeclared natural uranium metal. Iran dismantled the laser equipment in May 2003 and presented it to IAEA inspectors.[26]

Uranium conversion. Iran carried out a large number of laboratory- and bench-scale experiments between 1981 and 1993 involving multiple phases of the uranium conversion and fabrication process. Contrary to its previous statements, it had produced 'practically all of the materials important to uranium conversion', including enriched uranium metal, without notifying the IAEA.[27] Iran's production of uranium metal raised particular concern, since it has few uses outside a nuclear weapons programme.

Reprocessing. Iran conducted experiments at the Tehran Nuclear Research Centre from 1988 to 1992 involving the irradiation of uranium dioxide targets and the subsequent separation of a 'small amount' of separated plutonium. Iran admitted in October 2003 that it did not report either the experiments or the separated plutonium at the

[24] IAEA (note 22), p. 10.
[25] In Oct. 2003 Iran also admitted that it had failed to report the testing of centrifuges at the Kalaye Electric Company in 1999–2002 and the consequent production of small amounts of enriched uranium.
[26] IAEA (note 22), pp. 7–8.
[27] IAEA (note 22), p. 5.

time, as it was required to do under the terms of its safeguards agreement.[28]

The reactions to ElBaradei's November 2003 report to the Board were mixed. US officials and many independent analysts scoffed at its conclusion that there was 'no evidence' of a secret Iranian nuclear weapons programme. By contrast, Iranian officials said that the report vindicated their claim that the country's nuclear programme was entirely peaceful in nature. They argued that the safeguards infractions attributed to Iran were of a minor, technical nature and were bound to occur over decades of research work.[29]

On 26 November 2003 the IAEA Board of Governors approved a resolution 'strongly deplor[ing] Iran's past failures and breaches of its obligation to comply with the provisions of its Safeguards Agreement' and urging 'Iran to adhere strictly to its obligations under its Safeguards Agreement in both letter and spirit'.[30] The resolution warned that, should any further serious failures by Iran come to light, the Board would meet immediately 'to consider all options at its disposal, in accordance with the IAEA Statute'. However, the resolution stopped short of referring the issue to the Security Council for possible sanctions—a move that had been urged by the US Administration and strongly opposed by Iran. The then US Secretary of State Colin Powell reportedly was able to persuade only a few of the Board's 35 member states to go along with the administration's call for tougher action.[31] Many European states argued that steps recently taken by Iran warranted a more conciliatory approach—one that would bring into play a variety of incentives, such as the prospect of concluding a new Trade and Co-operation Agreement (TCA) with the EU, as well as coercive threats.[32]

[28] IAEA (note 22), p. 5.

[29] Fathi, N., 'Iran's leader says UN report removes suspicions of weapons', *New York Times* (Internet edn), 13 Nov. 2003, URL <http://www.nytimes.com/2003/11/13/international/middleeast/13IRAN.html>.

[30] IAEA, 'Implementation of the NPT safeguards agreement in the Islamic Republic of Iran', Resolution adopted by the IAEA Board of Governors, GOV/2003/81, 26 Nov. 2003, p. 2, URL <http://www.iaea.org/Publications/Documents/Board/2003/gov2003-81.pdf>.

[31] Sanger, D., 'Nuclear Board said to rebuff Bush over Iran', *New York Times* (Internet edn), 20 Nov. 2003, URL <http://www.nytimes.com/2003/11/20/international/middleeast/20IRAN.html>; and Weisman, S., 'US acquiesces to allies on new Iran resolution', *International Herald Tribune*, 26 Nov. 2003, p. 3.

[32] Fuller, T., 'A top EU aide backs Iran in feud over arms', *International Herald Tribune*, 18 Nov. 2003, p. 2.

Iran's signing of the Additional Protocol

On 18 December 2003, Iran signed an Additional Protocol to its NPT safeguards agreement.[33] The Iranian Government had indicated in the 21 October joint declaration that it would act in accordance with the Protocol's provisions, pending its formal entry into force. However, the government must submit the Protocol for ratification to the Majlis (Parliament), where some influential conservatives have vowed to oppose it.[34] On 21 May 2004 Iran submitted to the IAEA its initial expanded declaration under the Additional Protocol. Iranian officials stressed that the submission of the expanded declaration was a 'voluntary confidence-building measure', since the Additional Protocol had not entered into force.[35] They also insisted that all the IAEA's remaining safeguards compliance questions were being satisfactorily answered and that the Board of Governors should therefore vote to close the Iranian nuclear file at its next meeting.

The breakdown of the October 2003 suspension agreement

The October 2003 suspension agreement quickly became mired in a dispute over the scope of application of Iran's moratorium on enrichment. According to the E3, Iran was required to halt all uranium enrichment and related activities. Iran insisted that it was permitted to continue the testing and manufacturing of centrifuge components. It also announced that it intended to proceed with the production of uranium hexafluoride (UF_6) at its Esfahan conversion facility.[36]

On 18 June 2004, following another report from Director General ElBaradei that was critical of Iran, the IAEA Board of Governors adopted a resolution 'deploring' Iran's failure to provide the agency with 'full, timely and proactive co-operation'.[37] Among other meas-

---

[33] IAEA, 'Iran signs Additional Protocol on nuclear safeguards', IAEA News Center, 18 Dec. 2003, URL <http://www.iaea.org/NewsCenter/News/2003/iranap20031218.html>.

[34] For a discussion of the Additional Protocol and the domestic debate surrounding the Iranian Government's decision to sign it see chapter 5.

[35] 'Iran submits full report on nuclear program to UN nuclear agency', *Tehran Times*, 23 May 2004, pp. 1, 15.

[36] Uranium hexafluoride, either alone or in combination with hydrogen or helium, is the feedstock used in most uranium enrichment processes, including gas centrifuges.

[37] 'Implementation of the NPT safeguards agreement in the Islamic Republic of Iran', Resolution adopted by the IAEA Board of Governors, GOV/2004/49, Vienna, 18 June 2004, p. 2, URL <http://www.iaea.org/Publications/Documents/Board/2004/gov2004-49.pdf>.

ures, the Board's resolution urged that Iran implement fully its October 2003 pledge to suspend its uranium enrichment programme by halting the testing and manufacturing of centrifuge components. It also urged Iran to take additional steps to answer questions about its advanced gas centrifuge programme and about the source of enriched uranium particles found in environmental samples taken at three nuclear-related sites.

In response to the Board's resolution, Iran announced that it would resume its enrichment activities, including construction and centrifuge installation work at Natanz, under IAEA supervision.[38] It had initially argued that these activities were not part of the original suspension deal but later agreed to freeze them anyway at the request of the IAEA Board. Iran's decision to resume centrifuge production was followed by an announcement confirming that it would conduct uranium conversion experiments at its newly-built conversion plant at Esfahan. In August 2004 it began to convert 37 tonnes of uranium oxide ('yellowcake') into UF_6.[39]

These actions led to renewed European diplomatic efforts aimed at halting Iran's enrichment programme. There was particular disappointment in France, Germany and the UK that the October 2003 suspension agreement had unravelled. At the September 2004 meeting of the IAEA Board, the E3 supported a resolution calling for Iran to suspend all uranium enrichment activities immediately and to 'proactively assist the Agency to understand the full extent and nature' of its enrichment programme before the Board's meeting scheduled for the end of November 2004; otherwise, the Board would have to consider unspecified 'further steps'.[40] The resolution also called on Director General ElBaradei to make an assessment by the November meeting on whether he could give credible assurances that Iran had not produced or diverted nuclear material to a weapons programme.

[38] Mehr News Agency, 'Nation backs bid by government to resume construction of centrifuges: Legislators', *Tehran Times* (Internet edn), 27 June 2004, URL <http://www.tehrantimes.com/archives/description.asp?DA=6/27/2004&Cat=2&Num=031>.

[39] Two non-governmental experts calculated that theoretically this could produce *c*. 100 kg of weapon-grade HEU, which is enough for 5 crude nuclear weapons. Albright, D. and Hinderstein, C., 'Iran: countdown to showdown', *Bulletin of the Atomic Scientists*, vol. 60, no. 6 (Nov./Dec. 2004), p. 67.

[40] IAEA, 'Implementation of the NPT safeguards agreement in the Islamic Republic of Iran', Resolution adopted by the IAEA Board of Governors, GOV/2004/79, Vienna, 18 Sep. 2004, p. 2, URL <http://www.iaea.org/Publications/Documents/Board/2004/gov2004-79.pdf>.

The decision to set a deadline reflected a growing sense, in European capitals and elsewhere, that time was running out in that Iran was well along the road towards developing a capability to enrich uranium with few legal and technical obstacles in sight to prevent it from doing so.

At the same time, there continued to be a disagreement between the EU and the United States over whether to refer Iran to the UN Security Council. While this disagreement reflected underlying differences over means and modalities in their respective strategies for addressing the challenges raised by the proliferation of weapons of mass destruction (WMD), it also reflected differing tactical considerations.[41] Many European countries resisted the US demand for the Board to adopt a 'trigger mechanism' that would automatically require it to report Iran to the Security Council if Iran did not fully resolve all outstanding safeguards issues.[42] They argued that a referral of Iran's file to the Security Council, without the necessary diplomatic groundwork, would likely result in a deadlock on the Council over imposing sanctions, and that a referral might be counterproductive in that it could spur Iran to halt cooperation with the IAEA or even to withdraw from the NPT, following the North Korean precedent.

The IAEA assessment of Iran's safeguards implementation

On 15 November 2004 Director General ElBaradei sent to the IAEA Board the sixth in a series of written reports on the progress made by the agency in verifying Iran's implementation of its safeguards agreement with the agency.[43] The report came against the background of mounting pressure from Iran and the USA for the Board to make its forthcoming November meeting a decisive one in terms of either closing the nuclear file, as demanded by Iran, or referring it to the UN Security Council for further action, as urged by the USA. It included detailed summaries of the agency's findings that Iran had failed to report or declare to the agency eight different nuclear activities, including uranium conversion and enrichment experiments, as

[41] Eizenstat, S., 'Iran: a test for the European approach', *International Herald Tribune*, 14 Dec. 2004, p. 9.

[42] Reuters, 'US, Iran face off over EU nuclear draft: diplomats', *ABC News* (Internet edn), 23 Nov. 2004, URL <http://abcnews.go.com/International/print?id=276168>.

[43] IAEA, 'Implementation of the NPT safeguards agreement in the Islamic Republic of Iran', Report by the Director General to the IAEA Board of Governors, GOV/2004/83, 15 Nov. 2004, p. 23, URL <http://www.iaea.org/Publications/Documents/Board/2004/gov 2004-83.pdf>.

required under its safeguards agreement. It also described six instances in which Iran had failed to provide in a timely manner design information, or updated information, about nuclear fuel processing, storage and waste handling facilities.[44]

ElBaradei's report stated that there were three main safeguards compliance issues on which the IAEA was continuing to work with Iran in order to resolve them. The first was related to the source of the enriched uranium contamination found at some sites. Iran had blamed this on contaminated centrifuge components imported from a third country. IAEA investigators accepted that most of the contamination came from imported centrifuges but believed that the remainder may have originated in Iran.[45] If Iran had enriched uranium without first notifying the agency, this constituted a clear breach of its safeguards agreement. The second issue revolved around Iran's purchase of design plans for advanced centrifuges from a clandestine network of foreign intermediaries in 1995. Iran claimed that, because of a 'shortage of professional resources', it did not begin manufacturing work and mechanical testing of the centrifuge's composite rotors until 2002.[46] ElBaradei's report stated that the reason given by Iran for the delay did not 'provide sufficient assurance that there were no related activities carried out during that period'.[47] The third issue related to the date of plutonium separation experiments that Iran says were carried out 12–16 years ago, but which appeared to have been carried out more recently. In addition to these issues, the report also noted that IAEA investigators had not been able to come to a judgement about explanations provided by Iran for a number of other nuclear-related activities, such as experiments that it carried out in 1989–93 to produce polonium-210.[48]

On 29 November 2004 the IAEA Board of Governors adopted a much-anticipated resolution on the implementation of safeguards in Iran. The resolution noted that 'Iran's practices before October 2003 had resulted in many breaches of its obligations to comply with its

---

[44] IAEA (note 43), p. 22–23.

[45] IAEA (note 43), p. 23.

[46] IAEA (note 43), pp. 10–11.

[47] IAEA (note 43), p. 23.

[48] Polonium-210 is a short-lived, unstable element which has few commercial applications but has been used in the past as a neutron initiator for nuclear weapons. Iran said the experiments were aimed at producing radioisotope batteries. IAEA (note 43), p. 18.

safeguards agreement'.[49] It also noted that the 'Agency is not yet in a position to conclude that there are no undeclared nuclear materials or activities in Iran'.[50] At the same time, it welcomed Iran's decision to continue and extend its suspension of all uranium enrichment-related and plutonium reprocessing activities. While acknowledging Iran's breaches of its safeguards agreement, the Board's resolution did not declare it to be in non-compliance with either that agreement or the NPT.[51] The resolution also did not mention the possibility of referring the issue to the Security Council.

The new E3–Iranian suspension agreement

In the autumn of 2004 there were intense negotiations between Iran and the E3, supported by the High Representative for the European Union Common Foreign and Security Policy (CFSP), Javier Solana. The main issue was the E3's demand that Iran completely suspend its uranium enrichment programme.

On 15 November 2004, Solana and the foreign ministers of France, Germany, the UK and Iran met in Paris and signed a new suspension agreement.[52] The deal envisioned several steps. Iran undertook, as a 'voluntary confidence-building measure', to continue to extend its previous suspension to include all enrichment-related and repro-cessing activities.[53] The suspension would be sustained, under IAEA verification and monitoring, while negotiations proceeded 'on a

---

[49] IAEA, 'Implementation of the NPT safeguards agreement in the Islamic Republic of Iran', Resolution adopted by the IAEA Board of Governors, GOV/2004/90, Vienna, 29 Nov. 2004, p. 1, URL <http://www.iaea.org/Publications/Documents/Board/2004/gov2004-90_derestrict.pdf>.

[50] IAEA (note 49).

[51] According to Article XII.C of the IAEA Statute, the 'Board shall call upon the recipient State or States to remedy forthwith any [safeguards] non-compliance which it finds to have occurred. The Board shall report the non-compliance to all members and to the Security Council and General Assembly of the United Nations'. The full text of the IAEA Statute is available at URL <http://www.iaea.org/About/statute_text.html>.

[52] IAEA, 'Communication dated 26 November 2004 received from the permanent representatives of France, Germany, the Islamic Republic of Iran and the United Kingdom concerning the agreement signed in Paris on 15 November 2004', IAEA document INFCIRC/637, 26 Nov. 2004, URL <http://www.iaea.org/Publications/Documents/Infcircs/2004/infcirc637.pdf>. The text is reproduced in appendix A.

[53] The agreement specified these activities as follows: the manufacture and import of gas centrifuges and their components: the assembly, installation testing or operation of gas centrifuges; work to undertake any plutonium separation, or to construct or operate any plutonium separation installation; and all tests or production at any uranium conversion installation. IAEA (note 52).

mutually acceptable agreement on long-term arrangements'. The aim of the long-term agreement was to provide 'objective guarantees' that Iran's nuclear programme was exclusively for peaceful purposes as well as guarantees on nuclear, technological and economic cooperation between the EU and Iran and 'firm commitments on security issues'.[54] On 29 November ElBaradei reported that the IAEA had completed verification of Iran's suspension of its enrichment- and reprocessing-related activities.[55] This included the application of agency containment and surveillance measures at the Esfahan conversion facility and at declared centrifuge component production locations.

The Paris Agreement called for negotiations to be launched by a European–Iranian steering committee, which was also responsible for setting up working groups on political and security issues, technology and economic cooperation, and nuclear issues. The first meeting of the steering committee, which was attended by Solana, the British, French and German foreign ministers, and Hassan Rowhani, head of Iran's Supreme National Security Council, was held on 13 December 2004.[56] The first meetings of the working groups were held five days later. On 12 January 2005 the EU resumed the TCA negotiations with Iran which it had suspended in June 2003.[57]

The suspension deal came under some criticism, particularly in Israel and the USA. The main complaint was that the deal did not go far enough: Iran's moratorium on enrichment activities was a voluntary measure rather than a legal obligation; and its duration was directly linked to the duration of the negotiations between Iran and the E3 on the broader sets of issues.[58] The deal was also criticized for not requiring Iran to halt construction of the heavy-water reactor near

[54] IAEA (note 52).

[55] IAEA, 'Introductory statement by IAEA Director General Dr. Mohamed ElBaradei', IAEA Board of Governors, DG 25112004, 25 Nov. 2004, URL <http://www.iaea.org/News Center/Statements/2004/ebsp2004n016.html>. Iran requested an exemption from the suspension, stating that it wanted 'use up to 20 sets of [centrifuge] components for R&D [research and development] purposes and provide the Agency with access when requested'. It subsequently withdrew this request because of E3 opposition.

[56] 'Europeans restart talks with Iran', *International Herald Tribune*, 14 Dec. 2004, p. 5.

[57] The Nov. 2004 Paris Agreement stipulated that, once a suspension of Iran's enrichment programme had been verified, the TCA negotiations would resume. On the TCA see also chapter 6.

[58] Asculai, E. and Kam, E., 'Iran's slippery nuclear slope', Tel Aviv Notes, no. 117, Jaffee Center for Strategic Studies, Tel Aviv University, 22 Dec. 2004, pp. 2–3.

Arak.[59] This type of reactor is well suited for producing weapon-grade plutonium. There was speculation that Israel or the USA might launch pre-emptive military strikes against Iranian nuclear facilities in order to prevent, or at least slow down, Iran's development of a nuclear weapon capability.[60]

Progress of discussions between Iran and the E3

The talks between Iran and the E3 aimed at finding a durable settlement of the nuclear issue made little headway in the spring of 2005, and pessimism mounted on both sides. In a 10 March letter to the Council president, Solana and the British, French and German foreign ministers acknowledged that the negotiations with Iran were not progressing 'as fast as we would wish'.[61] The letter followed a briefing by Director General ElBaradei to the IAEA Board in which he noted that Iran had expedited the access of inspectors to nuclear material and facilities as well as to other locations of interest but that 'in some cases, the receipt of information is still pending, which in turn delays' the agency's work.[62]

The main point of contention continued to be the future of Iran's enrichment programme. The E3 insisted that Iran accept a complete and permanent cessation of the programme. They argued that this was the only meaningful 'objective guarantee' that Iran's nuclear activities were exclusively for peaceful purposes.[63] At the same time, the E3 recognized Iran's right to develop nuclear energy and pledged to facilitate Iran's access to nuclear technology and fuel. This included a

[59] Broad, W. and Sciolino, E., 'Iranians retain plutonium plan in nuclear deal', *New York Times* (Internet edn), 25 Nov. 2004, URL <http://www.nytimes.com/2004/11/25/international/middleeast/25NUKE.html>.

[60] Hersh, S., 'The coming wars', *New Yorker* (Internet edn), 24–31 Jan. 2005, URL <http://www.newyorker.com/fact/content/?050124fa_fact>.

[61] European Union, Council, [Text of letter to the president of the Council from Messrs Barnier, Fisher, Straw and Solana on Iran], 7222/05, 11 Mar. 2005, p. 5, URL <http://register.consilium.eu.int/pdf/en/05/st07/st07222.en05.pdf>.

[62] IAEA, 'Introductory Statement by IAEA Director General Dr Mohamed ElBaradei', IAEA Board of Governors, DG 28022005, 28 Feb. 2005, URL <http://www.iaea.org/NewsCenter/Statements/2005/ebsp2005n002.html>. A controversy arose in Jan. 2005 over the IAEA's request to make a follow-on visit to the Parchin military complex outside Tehran. Some reports have suggested that the complex could be part of a programme to develop conventional explosives for a nuclear warhead.

[63] European Union, Council (note 61), p. 4. They also noted that some Iranian activities, including quality assurance checks on centrifuge components, were causing 'serious concern'.

proposal to support Iran's acquisition of a light-water research reactor to replace the heavy-water reactor at Arak.[64]

Iran categorically rejected the European demand for a permanent cessation. Iranian officials complained that the demand violated the understanding reached in the November 2004 Paris Agreement.[65] They also emphasized that, as a non-nuclear weapon state (NNWS) party to the NPT, Iran was legally entitled to develop sensitive nuclear fuel-cycle facilities, including uranium enrichment, as part of its peaceful nuclear programme. They repeatedly stated that Iran would restart its enrichment activities, with appropriate assurances about their peaceful purpose, once the remaining safeguards issues had been resolved.[66]

In a May 2005 meeting of the Iran–EU Steering Committee, Iran proposed a comprehensive four-phase 'general framework' for resolving the nuclear issue.[67] One of the key elements of the proposal called for Iran to be allowed to maintain a limited uranium enrichment programme. This would include the assembly, installation and testing of 3000 gas centrifuges at the Natanz plant, to be accompanied by the negotiation of additional transparency and confidence-building measures beyond those mandated by the Additional Protocol. In exchange, Iran asked the EU to agree to sell it new light-water nuclear power reactors; provide a guaranteed supply of nuclear fuel; loosen export control regulations on the sale of advanced technology to Iran; and give greater access to the EU market for Iranian goods.[68]

The E3 agreed to study the Iranian proposal, amid speculation that there were divisions emerging in the negotiating positions of France, Germany and the UK over the enrichment issue.[69] The European

[64] European Union, Council (note 61), p. 3.

[65] Mehr News Agency, 'Iran will not be bound to commitments if EU officially demands halt to enrichment: Govt', *Tehran Times*, 5 Mar. 2005, pp. 1, 15.

[66] Mehr News Agency, 'Iran's nuclear activities will never be halted: Leader', *Tehran Times* (Internet edn), 30 Nov. 2004, URL <http://www.tehrantimes.com/archives/description. asp?DA=11/30/2004&Cat=2&Num=008>; and 'Iran says determined to resume uranium enrichment, Reuters, 24 Apr. 2005, URL <http://www.iranvajahan.net/cgi-bin/news. pl?l=en&y=2005&m=04&d=24&a=1>.

[67] 'General framework for objective guarantees, firm guarantees and firm commitments', 3 May 2005, text available at URL <http://abcnews.go.com/images/international/iran_eu_ objectives.pdf>.

[68] 'Progress needed in nuclear talks, Iran warns EU', *Global Security Newswire*, 20 Apr. 2005, URL <http://www.nti.org/d_newswire/issues/2005_4_20.html#9266DD60>.

[69] 'Chirac urges softening of EU stance on Iran', *Global Security Newswire*, 14 Apr. 2005, URL <http://www.nti.org/d_newswire/issues/2005/4/14/3af87c7e-dee5-46be-98ca-e768ff55 dac5.html>.

negotiators insisted publicly that their position that Iran must agree to cease its enrichment activities permanently remained unchanged.[70] However, they were reported to be struggling to find a formula that would keep the talks with Iran going without compromising on this position.[71] Iran's request for nuclear power reactors from Europe was also reportedly proving to be problematic for the E3.

With the negotiations facing serious difficulties, the E3 and the USA acknowledged the need to align their policies on Iran in order to give Iran additional incentives to abandon its enrichment programme. On 11 March 2005 US Secretary of State Condoleezza Rice stated that, if Iran agreed to renounce the programme permanently, the USA would drop its objections to Iran applying to join the World Trade Organization (WTO); it would also consider, 'on a case by case basis', licensing the sale of spare parts for Iranian civilian aircraft.[72] In return for this change in US policy, the E3 agreed to actively support US efforts to refer Iran to the Security Council if it resumed uranium enrichment.[73]

The convergence of the US and European approaches appeared to have little effect on Iran's determination to resume its enrichment programme. Iran rejected the US offer as insufficient and emphasized that the USA did not have a role to play in the talks with the E3.[74] Iranian negotiators warned their European counterparts that tangible progress had to be made in the talks to prevent them from breaking down. They indicated that Iran would restart operations at its uranium conversion plant in the summer of 2005 and eventually move ahead with its uranium enrichment programme, although they added that

---

[70] 'EU incentives not enough for nuclear deal, Iran says', *Global Security Newswire*, 18 Apr. 2005 URL <http://www.nti.org/d_newswire/issues/recent_stories.asp?category=nuclear#3 FB93BE9>.

[71] Khalaf, R. and Smyth, G., 'Euro trio's relief over Tehran's nuclear offer may prove short-lived', *Financial Times*, 21 Apr. 2005, p. 6.

[72] US Department of State, Bureau of Public Affairs, 'US support for the EU-3', Statement of Secretary of State Condoleeza Rice, Washington, DC, 11 Mar. 2005, URL <http://www.state.gov/secretary/rm/2005/43276.htm>.

[73] Sanger, D. and Weisman, S., 'US and European allies agree on steps in Iran dispute', *New York Times* (Internet edn), 11 Mar. 2005, URL <http://www.nytimes.com/2005/03/11/politics/11iran.html>.

[74] Islamic Republic News Agency (IRNA), 'Asefi says incentives will not persuade Iran to forsake rights', 12 Mar. 2005, URL <http://www.irna.ir/en/news/view/line-22/0503120791143125.htm>.

Iran would not resume its enrichment programme as long as a meaningful dialogue was under way.[75]

IV. Implications for the nuclear non-proliferation regime

The controversy over Iran's nuclear programme has raised serious questions about the effectiveness and viability of the nuclear non-proliferation regime. One particular concern arising from the Iranian case is that there is a structural weakness in the NPT: that Article IV, which gives NNWS parties an 'inalienable right' to import and develop materials and technologies for use in civil nuclear energy programmes, opens the possibility that an NNWS can covertly develop a nuclear weapon capability by putting in place the fuel-cycle facilities needed to produce weapon-usable nuclear material.[76] This has led to renewed interest in proposals for limiting uranium enrichment and plutonium reprocessing activities for civil nuclear programmes to a handful of fully transparent fuel-cycle facilities, operating under international control and monitoring.[77]

The concern about an inherent weakness in the NPT has been reinforced by revelations about the existence of a global black market in nuclear technology. The clandestine transnational network of companies and middlemen centred around Pakistan's leading nuclear scientist, Abdul Qadeer Khan, supplied sensitive nuclear technology and expertise to Iran and Libya, and possibly other states.[78] As a source for 'one-stop shopping', the Khan network circumvented many

[75] IRNA, 'Iran to quit talks if Europe turns out to be dishonest: Rowhani', 20 Apr. 2005, URL <http://www.irna.ir/en/news/view/line-22/0504200895153401.htm>.

[76] See, e.g., ElBaradei, M., 'Towards a safer world', *The Economist*, 18 Oct. 2003, pp. 43–44; Cirincione, J. and Wolfsthal, J., 'North Korea and Iran: Test cases for an improved non-proliferation regime?', *Arms Control Today*, vol. 33, no. 10 (Dec. 2003), pp. 11–14; and Levi, M., 'There is no absolute right to nuclear energy', *Financial Times*, 22 Sep. 2004, p. 15.

[77] In Feb. 2005, an international Expert Group appointed by IAEA Director General ElBaradei produced a report considering possible multilateral approaches to the most proliferation-sensitive parts of the nuclear fuel cycle—the production of new fuel, the processing of weapon-usable material and the disposal of spent fuel. IAEA, 'Multilateral approaches to the nuclear fuel cycle: Expert Group report submitted to the director general of the International Atomic Energy Agency', IAEA document INFCIRC/640, 22 Feb. 2005, URL <http://www.iaea.org/NewsCenter/News/2005/fuelcycle.html>.

[78] For a description of the Khan network's activities see Kile, S. N., 'Nuclear arms control and non-proliferation', *SIPRI Yearbook 2005: Armaments, Disarmament and International Security* (Oxford University Press: Oxford, 2005), pp. 552–55.

of the   traditional instruments, including export controls and international safeguards on nationally controlled fuel-cycle facilities and nuclear material holdings, designed to reduce proliferation risks.

These challenges are giving rise to innovative new measures aimed at preventing the spread of nuclear and other weapons of mass destruction and weapon-usable material. These include a new legal initiative, contained in UN Security Council Resolution 1540, which was adopted by a unanimous vote on 28 April 2005, as well as new ad hoc arrangements, such as the Proliferation Security Initiative (PSI). As the EU's anti-WMD strategy illustrates,[79] they are also giving rise to new multifunctional approaches to addressing proliferation concerns that involve the conditional application of the full range of political and economic—as well as military—instruments that the international community has at its disposal.

[79] See chapter 3.

2. The evolution of Iran's national security doctrine

Seyed Kazem Sajjadpour

I. Introduction

The literature on the security of Iran over the past quarter of a century shows clearly that Iran has been a security problem for the West and will continue to be so in the coming years, primarily in view of the issue of the nuclearization of Iran's security discourse. Interestingly, in this literature (including a plethora of books, journal articles and policy papers that represent opinion rather than pure analysis), the one single analytical factor that is vital to fathoming Iran's security behaviour—the evolution of its security doctrine from within—is almost completely absent. To put it another way, there exist two Irans with two contradictory interpretations of security and two different security narratives—'Iran from outside' and 'Iran from within'. This chapter addresses this gap by answering two basic questions: (*a*) how Iran is looked at in a security perspective from outside; and (*b*) how the evolution of Iran's security doctrine from within can be studied.

II. Iran's security behaviour seen from the outside

On the first question, the huge body of external literature on Iran as a security problem can be conceptualized as 'securitized', 'simplified' and 'static'. Iran is securitized in the sense that, given its existing political framework, it is seen as a threat by its very nature. The securitized perspective on Iran is an ideological projection and, like all ideological projections, is highly judgemental from the beginning and produces straightforward policy recommendations. The securitized perspective inherently suspects that Iran's intentions are malicious.

Simplification characterizes the literature on the security of Iran. A great deal of it depicts Iran as a simple entity, quite ignoring the complexities of a transitional society with a very rich historical experience gained over millennia and the complex social, political and economic determinants for its security behaviour. Sometimes the simplified presentation carries an element of analytical sophistication in applying rational models to infer the mentality and actuality of Iranian security practices. The problem with over-rationalization, however, is that nation states are not pure mathematical variables. The result of this simplification of Iran's security behaviour is at best guesswork detached from the realities.

Finally, the literature occasionally speaks of a static Iran, frozen in the images of the early post-revolutionary days. This depiction sometimes revolves around the elites, suggesting rigidity and radicalism in their mindset in the realm of security affairs.

The combined result is a picture of a dangerous entity which must be contained, controlled and changed. All these constructions contradict the reality and can be described at best as a misrepresentation and misperception of Iran.

III. Factors shaping Iran's security policy thinking

The alternative to these selectively designed and conflict-oriented analyses which originate from outside is to examine the evolution of Iran's security mindset from within. This requires an examination of the highly dynamic and interactive process between three concepts—place, people and policy—which reflect the complexities of a society that is searching for its proper and legitimate position in both the regional and the international settings.

Iran's geographical location has always been and remains the most important determinant of its security. Geography, which determines the final configuration of security settings, leaves Iran strategically lonely, sandwiched between different geographical regions and yet not really belonging to any of them. *Place* and its implications are central to the strategic thinking of Iran as a nation and to the thinking of its ruling elites who manage the security of a country in a volatile and uneasy region.

The second defining concept, *people*, refers to those who make national security decisions. Who are they? In what context do they make their decisions and what do they want or intend? Broadly speaking, the Iranian national security elites are of two distinct kinds—the core revolutionary generation and the second generation, with a gap of some 15–20 years between them. The former are now in their 60s and 70s and, although they are still attached to their missionary vision of transforming Iranian society through religious revolution, their thinking has matured with the cautious management of different security crises which provided useful learning experiences and boosted their self-confidence. The second generation, in their 40s and 50s, share the core values of the revolution with the older generation. What makes them different is their detailed knowledge and appropriate education. The older generation appreciates their skills and know-how and takes them seriously. Their professionalism, whether in the conduct of the multilateral dimension of national security affairs or in the administration of defence industry complexes, is of international standard. Interaction between the two generations takes place in a bureaucratic context characterized by mutual acceptance over the long term, trust and proven loyalty.

Because of the constitutional structure, as well as the inherent dynamism of Iranian society, decisions of a political and security nature are taken after a long process of careful examination and debate. This was reflected in the final decision to accept the IAEA Additional Protocol in 2003. The debate was both intense and transparent.

In the *policy* debate, the overriding issues at stake are the development of Iran, modernization of the economy, and the achievement of a balance between globalization and indigenous norms. This means that security is defined rather defensively, that is, Iran is jealously protecting itself. The siege mentality, which is a corollary of historical and geographical exigencies and a sense of being under constant pressure, particularly from the USA, has made the Iranian national security elites highly protective and above all careful not to jeopardize the country's security. A fair analysis of Iran's security behaviour at the time of Iraq's invasion of Kuwait in 1991 and the US invasions of Afghanistan in 2001 and of Iraq in 2003 attests to the difficulties of its security environment on the one hand and its prudent management of its security on the other.

The Iranian security elites follow a combined policy. Conceptually the aim is a combined strategy that incorporates economic, social and political elements, as reflected in the Fourth Five-Year Development Plan covering 2004–2009, currently in the final stage of approval in the Parliament (Majlis),[1] and the 'Twenty-year vision plan' approved by the Expediency Council. The definitions of security in the two documents are related, and both argue that security cannot be achieved unless a balance between social and political development is achieved.

Practically, Iran combines defence and diplomacy to secure its security. Diplomacy in both the bilateral and the multilateral forms is used intensively to provide Iran with the security it needs. The intense negotiations between Iran, the IAEA and three major European powers over the past two years clearly manifest Iran's intentions and capability for using diplomacy to reduce tension and build confidence.

A review of the evolution of the national security doctrine would be incomplete without a glance at the different periods into which the past 25 years can be divided. The 1980–88 Iraq–Iran War is the most important landmark. There are three periods—before, during and after the war. Before, revolutionary optimism and the lack of a proper national security apparatus defined Iran's security behaviour. During the war, which entailed a hard learning process, the Iranian elites came to define conclusions about the exigencies of Iran's international and regional setting and the importance of coordination in national security affairs. Where the latter was concerned, the setting up of the National Security Council with the amendment of the constitution in 1989 was the direct result of the lessons of the Iraq–Iran War. After the war, national security thinking showed the imprint of the war years in the meticulous calculations of costs and benefits in national security decisions, an understanding of the limitations as well as the potential of Iran's power, the centrality of diplomacy in national security, and the realization that a genuinely secure Iran will be the Iran that is developed economically, socially and politically.

This evolution has produced a generation of professionals that can be called an Iranian national security community with its own hierarchy, subculture, literature, and foreign policy and defence research institutes. More importantly, the rise of a national awareness and the established norm that Iran's security requires interactive international processes can be seen as one pillar of national security thinking. The

---

[1] 'Fourth Development Plan; Iran's roadmap to economic success', *Iran International Magazine*, June 2004, pp. 146–62, URL <http://www.netiran.com/?fn=artd(1773)=585f 5743ec4af005f9a9b90479d612be>.

other pillar in international relations discourse is very realistic: Iran cannot depend on others to provide its security.

The clear conclusion is that there is a cognitive gap between the Iran that is illustrated in the security literature in the West and the Iran that is trying to secure itself in a world that is full of uncertainty, a geographical setting where stability is lacking, and a domestic setting of unique dynamism and great complexity.

3. The EU Strategy against Proliferation of Weapons of Mass Destruction

Christer Ahlström

I. Introduction

On 21 October 2003 in Tehran, the foreign ministers of France, Germany and the UK secured a commitment from the Iranian Government to sign the IAEA Additional Protocol and begin the procedure for ratifying the protocol. Furthermore, the Iranian authorities declared that they had decided to voluntarily suspend all uranium enrichment and reprocessing activities. In return for these commitments, the three foreign ministers declared that—once the concerns of the international community as to the nature of its nuclear programme had been alleviated—Iran could expect easier access to modern technology and supplies. They also declared their willingness to cooperate with Iran to promote security and stability in the Middle East (including on the establishment of a zone free from weapons of mass destruction).[1]

The Tehran Declaration is sometimes misleadingly referred to as the 'EU 3' agreement.[2] It is important to bear in mind that the three foreign ministers travelled to Iran representing their own countries and not the EU as such. While the EU and its member states have expressed support for the actions of the three,[3] the EU itself did not assume the role of formal interlocutor in the subsequent developments in relation to the October agreement. That role remained primarily with the three countries participating in the October meeting in Tehran. It was only in the late autumn of 2004 that a more active EU role could also be seen in this process. At the Brussels European

[1] The Tehran Declaration—a statement by the Iranian Government and the 3 EU foreign ministers—is reproduced in appendix A.

[2] See, e.g., Einhorn, R. J., 'A transatlantic strategy on Iran's nuclear program', *Washington Quarterly*, vol. 27, no. 4 (autumn 2004), pp. 21–32; and Samore, G., 'Meeting Iran's nuclear challenge', Weapons of Mass Destruction Commission, Report no. 21 (Weapons of Mass Destruction Commission: Stockholm, 2004).

[3] See, e.g., European Union, 'EU high representative for the CFSP welcomes the announcements made today in Tehran on Iran's nuclear programme', SO216/03, Brussels, 21 Oct. 2003.

Council on 4 and 5 November, the Council of the European Union[4] declared that 'it confirmed that *the European Union and its Member States would remain actively engaged*—notably through the efforts of France, Germany, the UK and the EU High Representative—with the objective of achieving progress on the Iranian nuclear issue before the IAEA Board of Governors meeting starting on 25 November 2004'.[5] Furthermore, the Paris Agreement of 15 November 2004 states that it is concluded between the governments of France, Germany and the United Kingdom 'with the support of the High Representative of the European Union (E3/EU)' and the government of Iran.[6]

However, the EU has previously engaged with Iran directly as a collectivity. In December 2002 negotiations were opened on a TCA (a so-called 'mixed agreement', that is, an agreement with both political elements such as trade relations and economic elements such as development cooperation) between the EU and Iran. In the mandate for the negotiations with Iran, the Council stressed a linkage between the conclusion of such a TCA and agreement on separate instruments on political dialogue and counter-terrorism. Among the four areas identified for the political dialogue was non-proliferation, where the EU 'encourages Iran to sign, ratify and fully implement relevant international instruments'.[7]

As the negotiations between the EU and Iran opened up, information began to emerge on the scope of the Iranian nuclear programme, and questions were raised as to its nature. In June 2003 the Council noted with concern the outstanding questions raised by the IAEA and called on Iran to 'conclude and implement urgently and unconditionally an Additional Protocol' as a measure to demonstrate its peaceful intentions with regard to its nuclear programme.[8] It was also

[4] The Council of the European Union—the main decision-making body of the EU, representing the member states—is referred to hereafter as the Council. When meeting in certain configurations it becomes the General Affairs and External Relations Council (GAERC). Ministerial-level meetings in Council format have to be distinguished from the European Council—the meetings of heads of state and government.

[5] European Union, Council, 'Presidency conclusions, Brussels European Council, 4/5 November 2004', 14292/04, Brussels, 5 Nov. 2004, CONCL 3 (emphasis added).

[6] For the text of the agreement see European Union, 'Statement by Javier Solana, EU high representative for the CFSP, on the agreement on Iran's nuclear programme', SO304/04, Brussels, 15 Nov. 2004.

[7] European Union, Council, 'Conclusions of the 2437th Council meeting, General Affairs', 9717/02 (Presse 178), Luxembourg, 17 June 2002.

[8] European Union, Council, 'Conclusions of the 2518th Council meeting, General Affairs and External Relations', 10369/03 (Presse 166), Luxembourg, 16 June 2003.

made clear that progress on the TCA and the resolution of the nuclear issue were interdependent. The EU has since reiterated that conditionality, and the negotiations on the TCA have been put on hold pending a resolution of the nuclear issue.[9] At the Brussels European Council on 4–5 November 2004 it was declared that 'the negotiations on a Trade and Cooperation Agreement should be resumed as soon as suspension [of uranium enrichment facilities] was verified'.[10] Furthermore, in December 2004 the Council underlined that 'sustaining the full suspension of all enrichment related and reprocessing activities is essential for the continuation of the overall process'. It also stressed that a long-term arrangement resulting from the negotiations that began on 13 December 2004 'will have to provide objective guarantees that Iran's nuclear programme is exclusively for peaceful purposes'.[11]

The activities of the EU, and individual EU member states, in relation to Iran have been influenced to a significant extent by discussions within the organization on the formulation of a more coherent EU policy on non-proliferation of WMD. These activities culminated in December 2003 with the adoption of a Strategy against Proliferation of Weapons of Mass Destruction. The purpose of this chapter is to describe the development of this strategy and to discuss its contents and subsequent implementation.

II. The development of the EU WMD strategy

The year 2003 saw the EU countries give a much higher political profile to the issue of non-proliferation of weapons of mass destruction. There were several reasons behind this development.

One was the identification of proliferation of WMD as a threat to the EU countries. In June 2003, the EU High Representative for the CFSP, Javier Solana, presented the elements of a European Security Strategy in his 'A secure Europe in a better world'.[12] Solana's draft of

[9] See also chapter 6.

[10] European Union, Council (note 5).

[11] European Union, Council, 'Conclusions of the 2631st Council meeting, External Relations', 15461/04 (Presse 344), Brussels, 13–14 Dec. 2004.

[12] Solana, J., 'A secure Europe in a better world', Thessaloniki European Council, 20 June 2003, URL <http://ue.eu.int/ueDocs/cms_Data/docs/pressdata/EN/reports/76255.pdf>. See also Bailes, A. J. K., *The European Security Strategy: An Evolutionary History*, SIPRI Policy Paper no. 10 (SIPRI: Stockholm, 2005), pp. 22–28, available at URL <http://www.sipri.org/contents/publications/policy_papers.html>.

the strategy noted that WMD proliferation is 'the single most important threat to peace and security among nations'. A final and revised
version was adopted in December 2003: it described the proliferation
of WMD as 'potentially the greatest threat to our society'.[13]

Prior to 2003 it was not possible to speak of a coherent EU policy
on non-proliferation matters. The 1992 Treaty on European Union
(the Maastricht Treaty) established the CFSP 'covering all areas of
foreign and security policy', including all questions related to the
security of the EU.[14] Issues related to non-proliferation of WMD were
thereby in principle brought within the scope of the EU. The
Maastricht Treaty furthermore declared that member states shall
'work together to enhance and develop their mutual political
solidarity. They shall refrain from any action which is contrary to the
interests of the Union or likely to impair its effectiveness as a
cohesive force in international relations' (Article J.1(4)). However,
common EU policies in the area of non-proliferation were developed
cautiously. This was partly due to the diversity of the national
interests of member states: for example, in the nuclear field two of the
members are nuclear-weapon states, a majority are members of the
North Atlantic Treaty Organization (NATO), and a minority are non-
aligned and active within the New Agenda Coalition working for
nuclear disarmament. The discussions within the EU on non-
proliferation and disarmament were primarily carried out on a
technical level within two working groups under the Council—one on
non-proliferation (CONOP) and one on UN-related disarmament
issues (CODUN).

It was also problematic to say that the EU acted as a 'cohesive
force' in the field of non-proliferation of WMD. Internal regulations
on the different competences of the EU institutions and member states
could give a rather discordant impression in international
negotiations: on some issues the EU Presidency could speak on behalf
of all members, while on other issues it was the European
Commission that had this task. On other issues still the individual

---

[13] [European Union], 'A secure Europe in a better world: the European Security Strategy',
Brussels, 12 Dec. 2003, URL <http://ue.eu.int/uedocs/cmsUpload/78367.pdf>.

[14] Treaty on European Union, 1992 (Maastricht Treaty), Title V, Article J.1; see Title V,
Article 11 in 'Consolidated versions of the Treaty on European Union and of the Treaty
establishing the European Community (2002)', *Official Journal of the European Communities*, C325 (24 Dec. 2002), p. 5. See also McGoldrick, D., *International Relations Law of
the European Union* (Longman: London, 1997), p. 141.

member states spoke on their own behalf. Given this diversity, the development of common policies has often been piecemeal and ad hoc. On those issues where a common position was found, this position often covered the process rather than the substance of an issue. At times when the focus was on issues (such as nuclear disarmament) where there was no common view among the members of the EU, little if any progress was made. However, on issues where the members shared positions, the EU was able to act as a group and as such achieve results (e.g., the multilateralization of the 2002 Hague Code of Conduct against Ballistic Missile Proliferation (HCOC)).[15] This experience showed the members that the EU, when acting in a coherent manner, could actually have a significant impact in the field of non-proliferation of WMD.

One external factor that was to help in forging a common European policy on non-proliferation was the terrorist attacks of 11 September 2001. Although weapons of mass destruction were not used in these attacks, the massive destruction caused highlighted the prospects of a nexus between international terrorism and WMD. The most visible result of 11 September for the EU in the field of WMD was the launch in December 2001 of a 'targeted initiative' to respond effectively in the field of non-proliferation, disarmament and arms control to the international threat of terrorism.[16] This initiative was followed in April 2002 with a list of concrete measures.[17] The list identified four areas of action: (*a*) review and strengthening of the relevant multilateral instruments in the field of non-proliferation, disarmament and export control; (*b*) full implementation of export controls; (*c*) international cooperation in the field of protection and assistance against the use or threat of use of chemical and biological weapons; and (*d*) enhanced political dialogue with third countries in the field of non-proliferation, disarmament and arms control. It should be noted in this context that the increased attention being paid to non-proliferation of WMD among the members of the EU not only served the interest of addressing a threat to those members but also represented an act of

[15] On the role of the EU in the process of gathering support for the HCOC see Ahlström, C., 'Non-proliferation of ballistic missiles: the 2002 Code of Conduct', *SIPRI Yearbook 2003: Armaments, Disarmament and International Security* (Oxford University Press: Oxford, 2003), pp. 749–59.

[16] European Union, Council, 'Conclusions of the 2397th Council meeting—General Affairs', 15078/01 (Presse 460), Brussels, 10 Dec. 2001.

[17] European Union, Council, 'Conclusions of the 2421st Council meeting—General Affairs', 7705/02 (Presse 91), Luxembourg, 15 Apr. 2002, pp. II–VI.

solidarity with the USA, helping to foster engagement between the EU and the USA in general.

While the Council conclusions adopted in April 2002 underlined EU support for a large number of relevant processes and identified a number of actions, they did not establish a systematic programme for action at the EU level. The document did not identify the resources needed to implement such a programme or put in place a system to monitor the implementation of measures agreed. It essentially left it with the individual member state to decide which, if any, measure or action it would take.

The most important event that elevated non-proliferation from the technical to the political level within the EU was the military conflict over Iraq in 2003. This event demonstrated with clarity that solidarity within the CFSP still had to be developed. The question of how best to deal with Iraq's failure to carry out its disarmament obligations caused a significant split among the EU member states. A number of them, with the UK in the lead, sided with the US position that the use of force was the appropriate way to deal with Iraq. Other member states, with France and Germany in the lead, adopted the position that the UN-mandated inspection regime under the United Nations Monitoring, Verification and Inspection Commission (UNMOVIC) should be given more time to carry out its tasks.

The conflict over Iraq provided a strong impetus for the members of the EU to formulate a stronger, more coherent policy on the non-proliferation of weapons of mass destruction. The formulation of such a policy would serve several purposes. First, it would demonstrate both internally and externally that the members of the EU were capable of overcoming the divisions created by the Iraq war. Second, it would make it a little more difficult for member states to depart from the course of action they had committed themselves to follow and would, in a sense, 'lock them in' politically. Finally, for the EU to engage more systematically in issues related to non-proliferation of WMD, coupled with a pledge to work with the United States, would also serve the purpose of mending transatlantic relations, which had soured since mid-2002.

The first step was taken in the spring of 2003 by Sweden, which proposed EU action on non-proliferation. Then Swedish Foreign Minister Anna Lindh and her Greek counterpart, Giorgios Papandreou, outlined the proposal in an editorial in a major Swedish newspaper in

April. Under the headline 'How we can avoid a new Iraq', they argued that now was the time to counter the threat from WMD with preventive measures so as to avoid recourse to the use of force. They proposed the adoption of a new strategy to combat the proliferation of WMD within the EU.[18] The 14–15 April General Affairs and External Relations Council (GAERC) accepted this idea and commissioned the Council Secretariat to produce a draft document outlining the EU's strategic aims in the field of non-proliferation of WMD.[19]

The draft was presented to the Political and Security Committee (PSC) in June. The PSC agreed that the draft should be divided into two documents. The first would be a set of 'basic principles for an EU Strategy against Proliferation of Weapons of Mass Destruction'.[20] This document restated the EU's commitment to strengthen existing multilateral arms control, non-proliferation and disarmament processes, but was noteworthy for several other principles that were elaborated. It underlined the need for policies to be based on a common EU-level assessment of global proliferation threats, for which purpose the EU Situation Centre would prepare a threat assessment, 'using all available sources', that was to be maintained and continuously updated. Moreover, the intelligence services of the member states were to be instructed to engage in this process.

To enhance the credibility of the multilateral treaty regime the PSC underlined the need to reinforce compliance by enhancing the detectability of significant violations and strengthening the enforcement of the norms established in the treaties. Moreover, the PSC stressed that, where preventive measures (including the treaties, as well as national export controls) failed to prevent proliferation, 'coercive measures under Chapter VII of the United Nations Charter and international law (sanctions, selective or global, interceptions of shipments and, as appropriate, the use of force) could be envisioned'.[21]

The second document adopted in June was an Action Plan for the Implementation of the Basic Principles for an EU Strategy against

---

[18] Lindh, A. and Papandreou, G., 'Så undviker vi ett nytt Irak' [How we can avoid a new Iraq], *Dagens Nyheter*, 10 Apr. 2003, URL <http://www.regeringen.se/sb/d/1354>.

[19] European Union, Council, 'Conclusions of the 2501st Council meeting—General Affairs and External Relations', 8220/03 (Presse 105), Luxembourg, 14 Apr. 2003.

[20] European Union, Council, 'Basic Principles for an EU Strategy against Proliferation of Weapons of Mass Destruction', Note by the Council Secretariat, 10352/03, Brussels, 10 June 2003.

[21] European Union, Council (note 20).

Proliferation of Weapons of Mass Destruction.[22] The action plan described measures to be undertaken by the EU, grouped into two categories—measures for immediate action and measures to be implemented over a longer time frame. The seven measures identified for immediate action included: (*a*) firm engagement to promote the universalization and reinforcement of multilateral agreements; (*b*) rapid ratification and implementation of IAEA additional protocols by all the EU member states and acceding countries; (*c*) providing the IAEA with a budget increase sufficient to enable it to carry out its safeguarding tasks; and (*d*) the promotion of challenge inspections within the framework of the 1993 Chemical Weapons Convention (CWC).

Each task was to be accomplished before the end of 2003. It was also decided in the action plan to conduct a 'peer review' in all member states and the then acceding countries of their export control legislation in order to establish 'best practices' and to coordinate the EU's activities in this field better. The European Commission should coordinate this review and be assisted by a task force. Furthermore, the EU established a unit, known as the office of the Personal Representative of the High Representative on Non-Proliferation of WMD, within the Council Secretariat tasked with monitoring the implementation of the action plan as well as the collection of information and intelligence.

The penultimate step in the development of a strategy was taken at the Thessaloniki European Council on 19–20 June 2003 where a Declaration on Non-Proliferation of Weapons of Mass Destruction was adopted.[23] Drawing on the Basic Principles already established, the Council declared that the EU members 'are committed to further elaborate before the end of the year a coherent EU strategy to address the threat of proliferation, and to continue to develop and implement the EU Action Plan as a matter of priority'. Such a strategy was adopted at the European Council meeting in Brussels in December 2003.[24]

[22] European Union, Council, 'Action Plan for the Implementation of the Basic Principles for an EU Strategy against Proliferation of Weapons of Mass Destruction: note by the Council Secretariat', 10354/03, Brussels 10 June 2003.

[23] European Union, Council, 'Presidency conclusions, Thessaloniki European Council, 19–20 June 2003', 11638/03, Brussels, 1 Oct. 2003, POLGEN 55.

[24] European Union, Council, 'Presidency conclusions, Brussels European Council, 12–13 December 2003', 5381/04, Brussels, 5 Feb. 2004, POLGEN 2. The strategy itself is available at URL <http://ue.eu.int/uedocs/cmsUpload/st15708.en03.pdf>.

III. The substance of the strategy

The strategy consists of an introduction and three chapters. Chapter I describes the threats and challenges to international peace and security caused by proliferation of WMD. Chapter II outlines the response to this threat to be taken by the EU member states. Chapter III contains an action plan that specifies in some detail what actions EU member states should take in order to meet this threat.

The introduction begins by recognizing proliferation of WMD as a growing threat to international peace and security. It is a threat the EU cannot ignore. The EU 'must act with resolve, using all instruments and policies at its disposal. Our objective is to prevent, deter, halt and, where possible, eliminate proliferation programmes of concern worldwide'. Chapter I outlines developments that pose a threat to the effectiveness of the current control regime. Turning to the necessary responses, it notes that 'all the states of the Union and the EU institutions have a collective responsibility for preventing these risks by actively contributing to the fight against proliferation'. The implications of this recognition of a 'collective responsibility' cannot be overestimated in an organization that has a previous record of institutional infighting and where the different institutions guard their respective competences jealously.

Chapter II outlines how EU member states will address the threat of WMD proliferation. The leitmotif for these efforts is 'effective multilateralism'. It is recognized that 'a broad approach' covering a 'wide spectrum of actions' is needed. The members will be guided by the following elements: (*a*) a multilateralist approach to security, including disarmament and non-proliferation; a commitment to uphold, implement and strengthen the multilateral disarmament and non-proliferation treaties and agreements; (*b*) the 'mainstreaming' of non-proliferation into overall policies, drawing on all the resources and instruments available to the Union; (*c*) a determination to support the multilateral institutions charged with verification and upholding of compliance with these treaties; (*d*) a commitment to strong national and internationally coordinated export controls; (*e*) a conviction that the EU in pursuing effective non-proliferation should be forceful and inclusive, and needs to contribute actively to international stability; and (*f*) a commitment to cooperate with the United States and other partners who share their objectives.

At the same time, the EU will continue to address the root causes of instability, including through pursuing and enhancing its efforts in the areas of political conflicts, development assistance, the reduction of poverty and the promotion of human rights.

The strategy is clear in that it lays primary emphasis on political and diplomatic measures and resort to competent international organizations as the first line of defence against proliferation. If such measures were to fail, coercive measures under Chapter VII of the UN Charter and international law could be envisioned. Here it is stressed that the UN Security Council should play a central role.

The strategy also makes clear that the EU is 'committed to the multilateral treaty system, which provides the legal and normative basis for all non-proliferation efforts'. The EU should work for the universalization of existing disarmament and non-proliferation norms. It will assist third countries in the fulfilment of their obligations under multilateral conventions and regimes. It will also place 'particular' emphasis on a policy of reinforcing compliance with international treaties. It will seek improvements in the existing verification mechanisms and where necessary help to develop additional ones. The EU also declares its support for strengthened export control policies.

The strategy goes on to emphasize the promotion of a stable international and regional environment as a condition for the fight against the proliferation of WMD:

The best solution to the problem of proliferation of WMD is that countries should no longer feel they need them. If possible, political solutions should be found to the problems which lead them to seek WMD. The more secure countries feel, the more likely they are to abandon programmes: disarmament measures can lead to a virtuous circle just as weapons programmes can lead to an arms race.

This objective is to be pursued by means of fostering regional arms control and disarmament processes and by bilateral dialogue.

Chapter III outlines in concrete terms an action plan for the implementation of the strategy. The elements of the EU strategy should be integrated 'across the board'. It is recognized that there is a wide range of instruments available: (*a*) multilateral treaties and verification mechanisms; (*b*) national and internationally coordinated export controls; (*c*) cooperative threat reduction programmes; (*d*) political and economic levers (including trade and development policies); (*e*) interdiction of illegal procurement activities; and, as a last resort, (*f*) coercive measures in accordance with the UN Charter. While all are deemed necessary, 'none is sufficient in itself'. The EU should deploy those which are most effective in each case. It is emphasized that the objectives should be pursued making use of EU policies in different areas (e.g., trade agreements), so as to maximize their effectiveness.

The activities are divided into four main areas: (*a*) rendering multilateralism more effective by acting resolutely against proliferators; (*b*) promoting a stable international and regional environment; (*c*) cooperating closely with the United States and other key partners; and (*d*) developing the necessary structures within the EU.

The work for more effective multilateralism will mainly take the form of efforts to universalize and when necessary strengthen the treaties, agreements and verification arrangements on disarmament and non-proliferation. The EU will also consider how the role of the UN Security Council can be strengthened by providing independent expertise on verification and inspection (e.g., by investigating the possibility of a roster of experts in the field). A third measure is to enhance political, financial and technical support to verification regimes. In the field of export controls, the EU should work to strengthen export control policies and practices in coordination with non-EU partners of the export control regimes. It is also noted that the members should strengthen their own coordination in this area. They should work to enhance the security of proliferation-sensitive materials, equipment and expertise in the EU countries against unauthorized access and the risk of diversion.

To promote a stable international and regional environment, the EU members commit themselves to reinforcing cooperative threat reduction programmes with other countries in support of disarmament, the control and security of sensitive materials, and the development of facilities and expertise. For this purpose they also commit themselves to integrate their WMD proliferation concerns into the EU's political, diplomatic and economic activities and programmes.

The commitment to cooperate closely with the United States and other key partners entails, with respect to the former, adequate follow-up to the June 2003 EU–US declaration on non-proliferation,[25] coordination with respect to the latter and, where appropriate, joint initiatives with other key partners.

The undertaking to develop the necessary structures within the EU entails, among other things, organizing a six-monthly debate on the implementation of the strategy at the External Relations Council. Hence, in contrast to the 'targeted initiative' of 2002, the EU strategy has been endowed with an implementation mechanism. Reference is also made to the establishment, as agreed at the Thessaloniki European Council and described above, of a unit within the Council Secretariat entrusted with the monitoring of the consistent implementation of the EU strategy and the collection of information and intelligence, in liaison with the EU Situation Centre.

Finally, the normative nature of the WMD strategy should be noted. Under the CFSP, the instruments for the laying down of common policies are common strategies, joint actions and common positions.[26] For such instruments, Article 11(2) of the consolidated version of the Treaty on European Union lays down that the member states 'shall refrain from any action which is contrary to the interests of the Union or likely to impair its effectiveness as a cohesive force in international relations'.[27] Furthermore, the Council 'shall ensure that these principles are complied with'. The WMD strategy of December 2003, however, seems not to have been adopted in any of these three forms. This has led commentators to describe it as a non-legally binding *sui generis* document.[28] Yet, as noted above, the WMD strategy shares one characteristic with the formal documents of the CFSP in that its implementation is subject to a review process.

[25] European Union, 'Joint statement by European Council President Konstandinos Simitis, European Commission President Romano Prodi and US President George W. Bush on the proliferation of weapons of mass destruction', Washington, DC, 25 June 2003, URL <http://www.eu2003.gr/en/articles/2003/6/25/3156>. See also European Union, 'EU–US declaration on the non-proliferation of weapons of mass destruction, Dromoland Castle, 26 June 2004', URL <http://www.europa.eu.int/comm/external_relations/us/sum06_04/decl_wmd.pdf>.

[26] 'Consolidated version of the Treaty on European Union' (note 14), Title V, Article 12, p. 14.

[27] 'Consolidated version of the Treaty on European Union' (note 14), p. 14.

[28] Portela, C., 'The EU and the NPT: testing the new European non-proliferation strategy', *Disarmament Diplomacy*, vol. 78 (July/Aug. 2004), pp. 38–44.

IV. The implementation of the strategy

The adoption of an EU strategy against proliferation of weapons of mass destruction gives a clear signal that the members of the Union stand ready to act in a concerted way in this field. Of course, this readiness to act would not in itself be sufficient to fight proliferation. More important is the way in which this formulation of policy will guide the subsequent actions taken by the members of the organization. It has been said that one of the major challenges facing the EU is that of overcoming its 'long-standing reputation for being an organization of "much talk but little action" in addressing security challenges and threats'.[29] This section focuses on the measures taken by the EU under the WMD strategy.

Some measures were undertaken prior to the adoption of the strategy in December 2003. It was noted above that the Action Plan for the Implementation of the Basic Principles for an EU Strategy against Proliferation of Weapons of Mass Destruction, agreed in June 2003, described measures for immediate action by the EU. Among the seven measures identified for immediate action were a firm engagement to promote the universalization and reinforcement of multilateral agreements. In July 2003 the Council took a decision on the implementation of a common position on the EU's contribution to the promotion of the early entry into force of the 1996 Comprehensive Nuclear Test-Ban Treaty (CTBT).[30] The common position states that the EU shall encourage all states which have not yet done so to sign and ratify the treaty without delay. Priority is to be given to the 44 states whose ratification is necessary in order to bring the treaty into force. However, the common position does not include any novel thinking on how to overcome the obstacles the CTBT faces in relation to its entry into force.

The peer review of national export controls has also been carried out. A methodology for the implementation of the review was adopted in February 2004 on the basis of the proposals made by a task force. A programme of visits to all 25 member states by the task force was

[29] Dunay, P. and Lachowski, Z., 'Euro-Atlantic organizations and relationships', *SIPRI Yearbook 2004: Armaments, Disarmament and International Security* (Oxford University Press: Oxford, 2004), p. 44.

[30] European Union, 'Council Decision 2003/567/CFSP of 21 July 2003 implementing Common Position 1999/533/CFSP relating to the European Union's contribution to the promotion of the early entry into force of the Comprehensive Nuclear Test-Ban Treaty (CTBT)', *Official Journal of the European Union*, L192 (31 July 2003), p. 53.

completed by the summer of 2004. Oral and written interim reports were made to the Dual Use Working Party, containing observations on 'best practices' and areas where improvements might be made. A final report on the peer review was prepared by the European Commission and presented in November 2004.[31]

The action plan also identified the goal of mainstreaming non-proliferation policies into the EU's wider relations with third countries as a long-term measure. On 17 November 2003 the Council adopted a 'non-proliferation clause' to be included in agreements with third countries.[32] As the non-proliferation of WMD has been identified as a major concern, the EU will take this factor into account when considering whether or not it should develop its relations with a third country. Depending on the nature of the contractual relationship, the EU will aim for the inclusion of a non-proliferation clause. For *future* mixed agreements, the general rule is that such a clause should be included as an essential element in all agreements. For *existing* mixed agreements, the EU and its member states should aim to include a non-proliferation clause when the agreement comes up for renewal or revision. If there is a specific concern about WMD proliferation involving the third country, they could propose an amendment to the existing agreement. If no agreement is reached between the third country and the EU, the agreement could be denounced.

Where a so-called 'community-only' agreement exists or is to be negotiated with a third country, a non-proliferation clause cannot be included because of the lack of competence of the Community to negotiate in the field of non-proliferation of WMD. In such cases the Council could consider the conclusion of a 'parallel instrument' with the third country containing such a clause.

If a third country is found to be in non-compliance with a non-proliferation clause, the parties should as a first measure enter into consultations. If such consultations yield no results, the suspension of the agreement remains the last resort. Where wider EU conditionality

---

[31] The report in question is classified, but its main conclusions are apparently included in Working Party on Dual Use Goods, 'Recommendations further to the first stage of the peer review of Member States' Export Control Systems for Dual Use Goods conducted in the framework of the EU Strategy against the proliferation of Weapons of Mass Destruction', 15455/04, Brussels, 2 Dec. 2004.

[32] The 'non-proliferation clause' is published in European Union, Council, 'Note from the General Secretariat', 17 Nov. 2003, 14997/03 PESC 690, CODUN 45, CONOP 54. COARM 16+COPR 1, attachment to annex 1, available on the SIPRI website at URL <http://www.sipri.org/contents/expcon/wmd_mainstreaming.pdf>. It is reproduced in appendix B.

is concerned, the Council will invite the Commission to study the possibility of establishing a link between a country's non-compliance with its non-proliferation engagements and the suspension of Community assistance.

The non-proliferation model clause cannot, however, be regarded as mandatory: future non-proliferation clauses should be 'along the lines' of the text. In judging the merits of the non-EU signatory, the participation in relevant international instruments as well as the establishment of an effective export control system 'might be considered as essential elements on a case by case basis'.[33]

A non-proliferation clause has now been included in an agreement with Tajikistan.[34] Another agreement containing a slightly amended non-proliferation clause is the Association Agreement with Syria, which was initialled in October 2004.[35]

A more detailed common position on the universalization and reinforcement of multilateral agreements in the field of non-proliferation of WMD and their means of delivery was adopted by the Council on 17 November 2003.[36] The objectives of this common position are to promote universal participation in, and adherence to, five multilateral agreements—the 1968 NPT, the IAEA Additional Protocol, the 1972 Biological and Toxic Weapons Convention (BTWC), the 1993 CWC and the 2002 HCOC. Another objective is the early entry into force of the CTBT. The common position declares that the EU and its member states should pay particular attention to the question of enhancing the detectability of violations and should strengthen the enforcement of obligations established by these agreements. Particular emphasis should be placed on making best use of existing verification mechanisms and, where necessary, developing additional instruments. The member states also undertake to work to strengthen the role of the UN Security Council, 'which has the primary responsibility for the maintenance of international peace and security'.

---

[33] European Union, Council, 'Note from the General Secretariat' (note 32).

[34] European Commission, Directorate General External Relations, 'EU–Tajikistan: signature of the Partnership and Cooperation Agreement, Luxembourg, 11 October 2004', URL <http://europa.eu.int/comm/external_relations/tajikistan/intro/pca_11_10_04.htm>.

[35] On the negotiations with Syria see chapter 6, section VIII.

[36] European Union, 'Council common position 2003/805/CFSP on the universalization and reinforcement of multilateral agreements in the field of non-proliferation of weapons of mass destruction and means of delivery, Brussels, 17 November 2003', *Official Journal of the European Union*, L302 (20 Nov. 2003), p. 34.

The common position also specifies more detailed policy goals for the respective multilateral instruments. Space does not permit a detailed discussion of these goals here. Suffice it to note that, in respect of the NPT, the EU calls on all non-parties to 'accede unconditionally to the NPT as non-nuclear-weapon States'. It also declares its support for the Final Document of the 2000 NPT Review Conference and the decisions and resolution of the 1995 NPT Review and Extension Conference. The EU also considers that the Additional Protocol is an 'integral part' of the safeguards system. However, the common position is silent on the proposal put forward by the Nuclear Suppliers Group (NSG) and in other forums to make adherence to the Additional Protocol a condition of supply for nuclear goods and technologies.[37]

A question that has been on the agenda for several recent presidencies of the EU is the bringing into force of the IAEA Additional Protocol for all its members. The June 2003 action plan called for the rapid ratification and implementation of IAEA additional protocols by all EU member states and acceding countries. This was to be accomplished before the end of 2003. Given the role of the European Atomic Energy Community (Euratom), the procedure was that each member state ratified a dedicated agreement between itself and Euratom, and when all had done so the European Commission would ratify the Additional Protocol on behalf of all members with the depositary (the IAEA). In the event, the EU did not meet the 2003 deadline: it was not until 30 April 2004, the day before the enlargement of the EU with 10 new members, that the Commission formally notified the IAEA that the members of the EU were ready to apply the Additional Protocol.[38]

The EU has also taken steps to support the activities of the IAEA under the latter's Nuclear Security Programme. In March 2002, the IAEA Board of Governors approved a plan of activities to provide protection from nuclear terrorism. This plan aims to protect nuclear and other radioactive materials in use, storage and transport, and to detect the theft and smuggling of such materials. On 17 May 2004 the Council of the EU adopted a joint action on support for the IAEA's

---

[37] Anthony, I. and Bauer, S., 'Transfer controls and destruction programmes', *SIPRI Yearbook 2004* (note 29), pp. 742–43.

[38] European Union, 'Non-proliferation of nuclear weapons treaty: the Additional Protocol enters into force in all the member states', IP/04/602, Brussels, 6 May 2004.

Nuclear Security Programme.[39] The EU allocated the total sum of €3 329 000 to support the IAEA in carrying out three projects under this programme.

Support has also been provided to the Organisation for the Prohibition of Chemical Weapons (OPCW). In November 2004 the Council adopted a joint action on EU support for OPCW activities. The EU will allocate €1 841 000 to support action in the following three areas: (a) promoting universality of the CWC; (b) supporting the implementation of the CWC by states parties; and (c) international cooperation in the field of chemical activities.[40]

According to the EU strategy, the External Relations Council should have a six-monthly debate on its implementation. The first such debate was prepared in the PSC in June 2004. Before the PSC lay a progress report submitted by the Personal Representative of the High Representative on Non-Proliferation of WMD.[41] On 14 June 2004 the GAERC took note of the progress report and of the implementation of the EU strategy and welcomed the results achieved.[42]

The progress report outlines the different measures undertaken since the adoption of the strategy, but does not include any estimate of its impact. For example, it notes that several démarches have been carried out in support of the multilateral instruments but it does not explain how many states have been approached or, more importantly, if these démarches have yielded any tangible results. It is also noted that the 'WMD Strategy and its provisions are highlighted in the common statements which are made by the Presidency on behalf of the EU in relevant fora . . . These statements have emphasized the EU's commitment to the multilateral system, the importance of full compliance with existing treaty obligations and the willingness of the EU to work to strengthen these treaties where necessary'. The report

[39] European Union, 'Council joint action 2004/495/CFSP of 17 May 2004 on support for IAEA activities under its Nuclear Security Programme and in the framework of the implementation of the EU Strategy against Proliferation of Weapons of Mass Destruction, Brussels, 17 May 2004', *Official Journal of the European Union*, L182 (19 May 2004), p. 46.

[40] European Union, 'Council joint action 2004/797/CFSP of 22 November 2004 on support for OPCW activities in the framework of the implementation of the EU Strategy against Proliferation of Weapons of Mass Destruction, Brussels, 22 November 2004', *Official Journal of the European Union*, L349 (25 Nov. 2004), p. 63.

[41] European Union, Council, 'EU Strategy against Proliferation of Weapons of Mass Destruction: draft progress report on the implementation of Chapter III of the strategy', 10448/04, Brussels, 10 June 2004.

[42] European Union, Council, 'Conclusions of the 2591st Council meeting—General Affairs and External Relations', 10191/04 (Presse 196), Luxembourg, 14 June 2004.

came six months after the adoption of the strategy and (for obvious reasons) its general thrust is to describe the various issues under debate in the various EU working groups. There are few other concrete results to report on apart from those listed above.

The second six-monthly report was presented in December 2004.[43] Apart from listing activities undertaken in support of the implementation of the WMD strategy, the report prepared by the Personal Representative also contained a list of priorities for a coherent implementation of the strategy for the period up to 2008. The December 2004 GAERC took note of the report.[44] One of the more significant developments at this Council meeting was the adoption of recommendations as a result of the peer review of export controls.[45] It was recognized that the EU and its member states needed to develop a more proactive approach to the control of exports of dual-use items. Among the recommendations to strengthen the efficiency of the EU export control system were: (*a*) a commitment to investigate the possibilities for additional controls on transit and transhipment, (*b*) improvements in the sharing of denial information of export licences and consideration of the possibility of creating a database for the exchange of such information, (*c*) agreement on best practices for the enforcement of export controls, and (*d*) harmonization of implementation of 'catch-all' controls. The recommendations listed in the Council declaration were to be acted upon 'without delay'.

V. Conclusions

The events of the past three years have helped to forge a common EU policy in the field of non-proliferation of weapons of mass destruction. The strategy adopted in December 2003 is for the most part 'traditional' in the sense that it places primary emphasis on the prevention of proliferation by means of the universalization and implementation of multilateral agreements. It has been stated that the strategy 'allows the EU to keep a foot in both the past—the world of multilateral treaties—and allows some of its states to plan for the

[43] European Union, Council, 'Implementation of the WMD Strategy: six-monthly progress report. List of priorities for a coherent implementation', 15246/04, Brussels, 3 Dec. 2004.

[44] European Union, Council, 'Conclusions of the 2591st Council meeting—General Affairs and External Relations', 15460/04 (Presse 343), Brussels, 13 Dec. 2004.

[45] Working Party on Dual Use Goods (note 31).

disaggregated future'.[46] It should be noted, however, that the strategy contains some novel elements, such as the mainstreaming of non-proliferation objectives into other policy areas and the readiness to address the root causes of proliferation. In this sense, the 'holistic' nature of the EU strategy differs markedly from the WMD strategy adopted by the USA in December 2002: the latter focuses primarily on the pre-emptive use of force for counter-proliferation purposes and does not address the role of existing multilateral non-proliferation agreements, or the root causes of proliferation.[47]

It is obvious that the internal discussions within the EU on a WMD strategy have affected the approach of the 'E3' to Iran, as both the Tehran Declaration of 21 October 2003 and the Paris Agreement of 15 November 2004 reflect many of the key notions of the WMD strategy. The 2003 agreement indicates a willingness to address Iran's security situation—reflecting the commitment of the EU to address possible reasons why states may want to acquire WMD. The 2004 agreement reiterates rights and obligations under the NPT—reflecting the commitment of the EU countries to uphold non-proliferation agreements. The 2004 agreement links achievements in the nuclear field to the 'carrot' of trade and EU support for a possible accession of Iran into the WTO—reflecting the EU's commitment to mainstream non-proliferation into overall policies.

It is too early to make an overall assessment of the practical impact of the strategy. The fact that the initiative has been endowed with a review mechanism will serve to maintain a certain political momentum for it—a momentum that is likely to persist as long as the present focus on non-proliferation of WMD is maintained. The likely impact on third countries is also contingent on the role the EU plays as a collectivity in various parts of the world: if there is little or no role for the EU, the strategy will only have an impact if individual member states decide to follow it.

Previous attempts by the EU to formulate coherent policies in the field of non-proliferation and disarmament of WMD have been stymied by differences of view on the need for a balanced view on

[46] Littlewood, J., 'The EU strategy against proliferation of weapons of mass destruction', *Journal of European Affairs*, vol. 1, no. 1 (Aug. 2003), pp. 25–26.

[47] [USA], 'National Strategy to Combat Weapons of Mass Destruction', Dec. 2002, URL <http://www.state.gov/documents/organization/16092.pdf>. See also Boese, W., 'Bush administration releases strategy on WMD threats', *Arms Control Today*, vol. 33, no. 1 (Jan./Feb. 2003), p. 22.

these matters. While some member states have put the primary focus on non-proliferation, others have emphasized the need for disarmament measures. The current focus of EU activity lies almost exclusively on non-proliferation and has come about partly as a result of some member states being prepared to suppress their interest in disarmament—at least when working in an EU context. It cannot be excluded that a revival of calls for disarmament will weaken the coherent stand that the EU member states currently present in the field of non-proliferation of WMD.

The adoption of the EU WMD strategy has demonstrated that the EU and its member states are capable of finding common ground on important issues on the contemporary security agenda. The previous lack of such a common platform signified to non-members that they could not really anticipate that the EU would act in a coherent manner. Today this situation has changed, and with the advent of a common strategy greater expectations of EU action follow as well.

4. The nuclear controversy in the context of Iran's evolving defence strategy

Jalil Roshandel

I. Introduction

Debates over Iran's nuclear weapons programme are currently making headlines. The media in the United States are paying extraordinary, almost hourly, attention to a whole range of issues related to Iran, from economic sanctions to the talks with the 'E3' (France, Germany and the United Kingdom). In Europe there is even more interest in helping Iran avoid a United Nations Security Council decision on its nuclear programme. In the Middle East, Iran is the centre of attention not only because of internal developments, which could significantly influence the fate of democracy in the region, but also because of the concern expressed by Israel and the likelihood of a pre-emptive strike against Iran's nuclear installations. If another war happens in the Middle East it will have a devastating impact on every country in the region, if not the whole world. Israel's concern about Iran is twofold. It arises, first, because ever since the 1979 Islamic Revolution Iran has rejected Israel's right to exist and, second, because it now claims to be mass-producing the Shahab-3 ballistic missile, which is capable of hitting Israel.

This chapter seeks to answer the question why Iran should expose itself to so much international attention and criticism. It places the current nuclear controversy in the context of Iran's defence and national security strategies. To cast light on these and on their evolution, it looks first at the structure and role of Iran's defence forces. It then examines what their development over time reveals about Iran's perceptions of the internal and external security challenges facing it, and how it has responded to these perceived threats. Here, the chapter inverts traditional approaches that begin by attempting to identify a hierarchy of threat perceptions. It pays particular attention to how recent developments in the regional security environment, including the US-led occupations of Afghanistan and Iraq, have shaped Iran's emerging strategy of 'active neutrality' and have affected its thinking about the role of deterrence in the country's defence doctrine.

II. The legacy of the Iraq–Iran War

Shortly after the Islamic Revolution, when war with Iraq broke out in September 1980, the Islamic Republic of Iran was both internally and externally vulnerable and had no real defence strategy. It was neither expecting nor prepared for the war and was taken by surprise when Iraqi troops attacked and easily occupied parts of its oil-rich southwest. The system of alliance with the USA was broken as a result of Iran's revolutionary fervour, and this was followed by a second blunder—the decision to join the Non-Aligned Movement. As a consequence, the entire 1980–88 Iraq–Iran War was fought without any significant military support from a friendly state, with the exception of Syria, which pursued its own regional interests by offering some tactical support. Politically, too, Iran had very few friends and soon entered into a phase of international isolation while following specific goals within the Islamic world.

Iran's new political and geo-strategic situation in the region and its role as a state that claimed leadership in the Muslim world required the planning of a different military strategy and defence doctrine, and the revolutionaries were unprepared for this. Goals such as exporting the revolution were far more difficult to achieve with a war-torn army and an economy that was all too dependent on oil. However, the Iraq–Iran War was an important experience. It highlighted the overwhelming weakness and shortcomings that needed to be addressed both during and after the war. More than anything else it proved that, in the absence of any system of alliances, Iran needed more aggressive 'defensive' weapons or some type of WMD that could deter a ruthless enemy such as Saddam Hussein. During the war Iraq had used its Scud missile capability extensively to hit Tehran and even some central and northern regions of Iran, while Iran was barely able to respond to the missile attacks. Towards the end of the war Iraq also used chemical weapons and inflicted severe casualties on Iranian troops and civilians who had no experience of war or lethal chemical weapons.

Despite the fact that revolutionary Iran had initially rejected the need to have advanced weapon systems, and had cancelled its order for US airborne warning and control system (AWACS) aircraft as well as nuclear technologies ordered under the Shah, by the mid-1980s it was clear that the regime had shifted from rejecting advanced technologies to appreciating their potential value, and a desire to obtain WMD emerged. The reason for this was simple, convincing and concrete: had Iran been in possession of them, the Iraq–Iran War could have been avoided or ended with much more positive results for Iran, or would have lasted a much shorter time than eight years. In addition, the unfinished nuclear power plant at Bushehr—the construction of which had been initiated by the Shah in the 1970s—reminded many people of the Shah's ambitious plans to make Iran a regional power, at a time when Iran was unable even to take significant steps towards finishing the construction of the plant.

Today, 25 years later, Iran has established its basic capabilities for highly advanced technologies and is committed to producing nuclear fuel for its planned power reactors. Although it insists that its nuclear programme is peaceful and it has no desire to produce nuclear weapons, it is failing to convince the concerned countries of the international community about its intentions. At the same time, Iran has made gradual but indisputable improvements in key areas of military technology. These developments have influenced Iran's defence doctrine. It should be noted that in a period of approximately one year the range of Iranian-produced ballistic missiles increased from 1300 to 2000 kilometres. Iranian leaders claim that the country has 'the power to fire missiles to a range of 2000 kilometres', which means that they can hit Israel and parts of South-Eastern Europe.[1] Suspicions about the existence of a political will to equip these 'strategic missiles' with nuclear warheads seem rational as long as Iran cannot convince the international community that it has no intention to develop nuclear weapons. However, between political desire and technological feasibility there is a big gap, and Iran does not seem likely to be able to achieve a very strong capability in the short term.

III. Iran and deterrence

Israel and the United States continue to pressure Iran to freeze all its sensitive nuclear fuel-cycle activities, including its uranium enrichment programme, fearing that these will lead to a capability to

---

[1] Rafsanjani, H. (former Iranian president), 'Aknoon Bayad beh fekr taskhir faza bashim' [Think about conquering the space, now], *Aftab Yazd* [Persian daily], 6 Oct 2004, p. 2 (in Farsi), URL <http://www.aftabyazd.com/HtmlFile/MainArchive.htm>. This statement was also quoted by the international media: see, e.g., *Jordan Times*, 6 Oct. 2004.

produce a nuclear weapon. They believe that Iran's declared peaceful nuclear programme is only a cover for developing such weapons. China and Russia have both taken a more opportunistic approach following their own long-term interests. Iran, on the other hand, has been carefully cooperating with the IAEA, hoping to convince the agency about the peaceful nature of its programme. In return for Iran's agreeing to suspend its uranium enrichment programme and to provide 'objective guarantees' about the peaceful nature of its nuclear programme, the E3 have offered civilian nuclear technology, including access to nuclear fuel, increased trade and help with Iran's regional security concerns. Iran agreed, but controversies emerged and IAEA verification is under way. In the meantime comprehensive negotiations between Iran and the three European countries have started.[2]

Ballistic missiles in Iran's strategy

Despite the ongoing negotiations on nuclear issues, Iran's efforts to develop more advanced ballistic and cruise missile technology remain a source of major concern. The centrepiece of these efforts is the 1300–1500 km-range Shahab-3 ballistic missile, which is based on North Korea's No Dong missile technology.

Confusing and ambiguous messages from Iranian decision makers have raised the level of international concern and uncertainty about this and other missile programmes. For instance, according to former President Hashemi Rafsanjani, 'experts know that a country that possesses this [strategic missile] can obtain all subsequent stages' in their development.[3] Rafsanjani's statement was corroborated by an anonymous senior Western intelligence analyst, who claimed that 'Iran has obtained the expertise and equipment to produce variants of North Korean engines for the Shahab-3' and that 'Teheran has sought this capability for a long time and we believe they have achieved it'.[4] This report stated that Iran had obtained only about 20 North Korean liquid-fuel engines for its locally produced Shahab-3 missiles and hence cannot begin serial production. However, according to Defence

---

[2] See chapter 3.

[3] Islamic Republic News Agency (IRNA), 5 Oct. 2004. Rafsanjani was president of Iran from 1989 to 1997 and has served as chairman of the Expediency Council since 1997.

[4] 'Iran produces engines for Shihab-3', Middle East News Line, 10 Nov. 2004, URL <http://www.menewsline.com/stories/2004/november/11_11_1.html>.

Minister Ali Shamkhani, Iran is capable of 'mass-producing' these missiles, which he said are 'capable of hitting Israel', at a rate comparable to the production of the Paykan (a domestically produced car). While the motivation for such claims probably lies in recent Israeli threats to consider the military option to stop Iran's nuclear programme, Shamkhani also emphasized that his task is 'developing defence capabilities' and that he has surpassed his objectives.[5]

It appears that Iran is geared to a psychological war to deter the Israeli threat through its Shahab-3 missiles. In the words of the commander-in-chief of the Islamic Revolutionary Guard Corps (IRGC), Major General Yahya Rahim Safavi, Iran will break 'the Zionist regime into pieces' if Israel targets the Iranian nation.[6] Similarly, Foreign Minister Kamal Kharrazi stated: 'When there is a threat, you have to take it into consideration and be prepared to react. We are prepared'.[7]

Two main arguments can to some extent justify or explain the claims of Shamkhani or similar claims by Rafsanjani. First, Iran feels very vulnerable to a not-so-improbable pre-emptive military strike on its nuclear facilities by Israel and is therefore speeding up the development of its defensive capabilities despite uncertainties about the range, targeting and effectiveness of medium-range missiles armed with conventional warheads, such as the Shahab-3. If this is correct then Israel could be targeted by Shahab-3 missiles launched from Iranian territory. However, because of the uncertainty of targeting, Palestinian areas would be vulnerable. A second motive for such claims could be simply bargaining purposes. Iran is in fact using all its cards, including exaggerating the scope of its ballistic missile system, to send a clear message to the West and the entire world to pay attention to Iran. It is, as Graham Fuller correctly put it, 'the centre of the universe'.[8]

[5] Defence Minister Ali Shamkhani, quoted by the Iranian Student News Agency (ISNA), in 'Iran boasts it can mass-produce Shahab-3 missile', 9 Nov. 2004 (source AFP), URL <http://www.turkishpress.com/news.asp?id=33260>.

[6] IRNA, 'IRGC commander warns Zionist regime against targeting Iran', 11 Aug. 2004, URL <http://www.globalsecurity.org/wmd/library/news/iran/2004/iran-040811-irna04.htm>.

[7] Kyodo/IRNA, 'Iranian FM sees Israel as a threat, denies nuke arms program', 4 Oct. 2004, URL <http://www.globalsecurity.org/wmd/library/news/iran/2004/iran-041004-irna01.htm>.

[8] Fuller uses this phrase in the title of his book. Fuller, G., *The Center of the Universe: The Geopolitics of Iran* (Westview Press: Boulder, Colo., 1991).

Iran's missile system does not yet constitute a strong deterrent to Israel. A missile system per se is not a defensive system and it cannot alone deter an adversary, especially if it only carries conventional warheads. Israel has purchased advanced versions of the Patriot anti-missile system from the USA, and its own Arrow-2 missile defence system is designed to engage missiles such as the Shahab-3, which Iran has yet to deploy in significant numbers. In the long term the Shahab-3, if equipped with nuclear warheads, could be a potent strategic system against which no missile defence system would be sufficiently effective. However, as mentioned above, between intentions and capability there is a big gap, and it is not certain that Iran can bridge that gap.

IV. The evolution of Iran's security forces and defence mentality

The Islamic Revolutionary Guard Corps

With the downfall of the monarchy in 1979, the generals of the Shah's armed forces left Iran or were purged and executed, and the regular armed forces were left disorganized. As a result Iran was defenceless during the war with Iraq. With the establishment of the IRGC after the revolution, the remaining armed forces came under scrutiny even more and faced further challenges. The IRGC was organized in a way that permitted more selective military recruitment: its troops and commanders were recruited among the masses and their allegiance to Islamic values and revolutionary ideals were far more important than their military expertise. At the very beginning, it was like a para-military force that was attempting to learn warfare by trial and error rather than acquiring expertise and effectiveness through education and training. By drawing on almost all segments of society and encouraging them to offer their lives to defend Iran, and in the absence of any strategy, Iran was in effect following a total defence strategy. Upper-class participation, however, was limited or only financially significant; the upper class would always find a way not to send their sons to the front but would attempt to buy special treatment for them—often by illicit and corrupt means. From the start this made the IRGC and its related organization vulnerable to external illegal and corrupt influences.

The IRGC expanded rapidly during the war. As a parallel military and defence establishment, it required an independent general staff and related military administrative personnel. In practical terms it was an expensive institution. Its creation was partly justified by its unquestioning religious and revolutionary loyalty to the regime, its (accomplished) mission to fight the Iraqi aggressors, and its criticism of the formal army that had failed to respond to the Iraqi aggression during the presidency of Abolhassan Bani Sadr (1980–81). Bani Sadr himself was accused of weak performance in leading the Iranian troops in war, and Iran's spiritual leader, Ayatollah Khomeini, therefore stripped the presidency of the power of commander-in-chief and transferred that power to his own office.

It was in these circumstances that the IRGC emerged, much like the Chinese People's Liberation Army, with the dual task of containing all three branches of the formal armed forces—which might have remained loyal to the Shah or Bani Sadr—as well as defending Iran against any threat, internal or external. Years of trial and error effectively transformed the IRGC into a rival force to the Iranian Army, with specific functions, although both forces were and still are under the one defence ministry.

Unlike the formal army, the rank and file in the IRGC were selected from among the masses who had participated actively in the revolution and remained active within the revolutionary committees until the beginning of the war with Iraq in 1980, and had then moved fairly rapidly upwards through a system of rewards and punishment devised to keep them further committed. Most IRGC members received their military or equivalent ranks during and after the war with Iraq. Religiously motivated, this force was able to operate under very difficult circumstances; it was prepared to work under severe restrictions and yet have few expectations of the system. The organizational structure of the IRGC supported a variety of internal and external actions, from overt operations against internal uprisings to covert cooperation with revolutionary forces outside Iran, and even the highly secret tasks of repairing, replicating, testing or operating weapon systems or equipment which Iran could not procure from international markets under the US and European sanctions.

This privileged position gave the IRGC almost free rein to intervene whenever and wherever needed. It could intervene in public affairs for many reasons, including (but not exclusively) when 'political disputes among the regime's various factions get out of hand',[9] for military training and exercises, for handling the submarines later purchased from Russia, or simply for economic activities such as installing gas pipelines in the mountainous region of Kurdistan where no private-sector contractors were able to work. Militarily, it was believed to be well prepared to 'safeguard the country, nation and the Islamic Revolution'.[10]

Many technological achievements were initiated by the IRGC rather than the formal army. For instance, in October 1997, after the purchase of the two submarines from Russia, at a time when their capability and efficiency were under question, Defence Minister Shamkhani announced that the IRGC had produced batteries for use by the submarines, emphasizing that 'acquiring the technology to produce batteries for Kilo Class submarines, is a major step towards achieving self sufficiency by the Iranian defence industries'.[11] Gradually, the IRGC has been transformed into an all-round, resourceful military force that is trusted with the responsibility of guarding the revolution and helping the clerics or the elites in the day-to-day enforcement of their power, while Iran's constitution entrusts the regular army with safeguarding Iran's territorial integrity and political independence.

The Basij: a 'human shield' against internal and external threats

In the course of the war with Iraq a third, paramilitary force emerged—the Basij, organized and staffed by civilians to provide support to the IRGC and the regular military. It recruits its members from mostly under-age high-school student volunteers and vigilante groups from both urban and rural areas, and is the third component of Iran's military human shield and security force. It is often praised for its omnipresence in internal affairs, although elite groups from the Basij combined with selected members of the IRGC such as the Ashura Brigades force may be involved in external affairs as well. At different stages of the war with Iraq, as members of the Basij, '550,000 students participated and 36,000 were killed', and significant

[9] *Al-Moujez-an-Iran*, vol. 6, no. 16 (Dec. 1996); and Iran Briefing Index, URL <http://www.caisuk.com/almouj.htm>.

[10] IRGC Commander Brigadier General Yahya Rahim Safavi, quoted by IRNA, 'Leader: no world power can overpower Iranian nation', 15 Sep. 2002.

[11] IRNA, 14 Oct. 1997.

support, motivation and incentives were given to young volunteers and vigilante groups to join the Basij.[12] This paramilitary group could be lined up in any emergency situation, including domestic uprisings and unrest or any event that threatened national security.

In the event of a new war the armed forces of Iran would engage first, followed by the IRGC and the Basij. During peacetime the Basij has been more involved in domestic missions such as the spiritual purification of the people, the Islamization of society, night-time control of road junctions and streets in cities, and policing duties wherever young people may gather, including in the universities and at weekend and summer activities for young people.[13]

It is interesting to note that both the IRGC and the Basij have been shaped in such a way as to function in conditions of severe hardship and to be prepared to do anything, go anywhere, and work under any circumstances. Although their loyalty to the Islamic value system is at times based on obedience to command, in general it goes beyond personalities and has been specifically formed around a deeply rooted and tested belief in Islam, its value system and the Islamic regime. This value-oriented belief favours absolute obedience to orders received without questioning the legitimacy, the legality or the basis of the order. Orders are executed because of religious conviction and not because they are issued by a legal and rights system for which the person concerned has voted.

This force was created in response to a key concern about internal conditions leading to an uncontrollable situation. Despite its seeming stability, Iranian society is in deep trouble. Profound disillusionment, frustration and a lack of consent to domestic policies, along with the suppression and control of young people, have to be seen as the core reasons why Iran continues to devote a significant portion of the national budget to maintaining these separate parallel forces.

Much effort has been put into demonstrating that the Iranian armed forces (the formal army, the IRGC and the Basij combined) are prepared to meet external threats. This is of course true of all nations of the world, but, considering the quality and the structure of the

[12] IRNA, 14 Oct. 1997.

[13] In a meeting with high-school students, Khatami praised the Basij for its continuous support and presence in the war with Iraq and in the country, saying 'Basij is beyond peace and war'. Iranian Students News Agency (ISNA), quoted by the Iranian daily *Hamshahri*: 'Basij Mazhar-e Ghanoongarayee, Azadi va Pishraft ast' [Basij, the symbol of lawfulness, freedom and development], 30 Oct. 2004, URL <http://www.hamshahri.net> (in Farsi).

forces in Iran, the way they have reacted to internal episodes and the way in which their respective roles have evolved, it is easy to conclude that they are on permanent alert to intervene in all conceivable forms of internal as well as external threat. General Mohammad Hejazi, chief commander of the Basij, recently stated that 'Basij forces could be deployed in between two to eight hours while Israel can deploy its quick reaction troops in 24 hours'. He also compared the Basij to many armies of the world and claimed that it alone would be able to conduct a 'total defence'.[14] Hejazi was speaking on issues related to Tehran University students: this statement seems to have more internal than external implications.

V. The internal dimensions of the threat to survival: regime security

Preserving the Islamic nature of the Iranian regime has always been an issue, and any attempt to transform Iranian society culturally is therefore perceived as a threat to the survival of the Islamic system. During the early years after the revolution, such attempts might have been less threatening or might have been considered to be less than a threat to the survival of the regime, but any signs of such attempts have been meticulously monitored and resisted at all times. This is one of the basic reasons why the Basij was created.

Several internal and external incidents indicate the vulnerability of the regime—the election of President Mohammad Khatami in 1997, the student uprising in 1998 and its fifth anniversary in 2003. The level of threat was even higher when US and Coalition forces attacked Afghanistan in October 2001. Around that time a considerable number of people wished that the USA would also target Iran, thinking that the end of the Taliban regime in Afghanistan would end the Iranian equivalent of the Taliban as well. This wish was disappointed when US troops attacked Iraq in March 2003, but has remained stronger outside Iran. With the war on Iraq, people who had initially been happy to see their arch-enemy Saddam Hussein gone at the expense of the USA soon recognized that the price they would have to pay in the event of an attack to Iran would be much higher than expected.

---

[14] Iranian Labour News Agency (ILNA), [Twenty-five years of Basij activity documents], 20 Nov. 2004, quoted by the *Javan Daily* website, URL <http://www.javannewspaper.com/1383/830830/internal.htm> (in Farsi).

Revolution, war and chaos are not what people always want, and young Iranians have perhaps the right assessment of the situation. They want to reform the system from within, regardless of the fact that this might be seen as a threat to the survival of the regime. The immediate reaction to this threat has always been more repression and restrictions on access to external information sources, coupled with an appeal to the Basij as ultimately the most effective force to confront internal surprises.

The current commander of the IRGC, Brigadier General Safavi, who was once the commander in chief of the Basij, speaking at the 13th gathering of IRGC commanders exactly one year before 11 September 2001, expressed his belief that this mass volunteer force, equipped with 'pure Islamic thought', was prepared to 'defend the revolution and Imam Khomeini's ideals with foresight and armed with cultural tools'. Safavi was in fact referring to a major concern in Iranian society today, which is the fear of internal transformation among the revolution's second generation. The threat of a dramatic change in society has been strongly felt in Iran since the student uprising of 1998. Safavi also emphasized that 'pure Islamic thought' will confront the 'Western way of thinking' which aims to dilute the religious beliefs of the people.[15]

In addition to the Basij, which is probably not powerful enough to confront a rapid deterioration of the internal security situation, there are special riot control forces often known as Lebas Shakhsiha (literally 'dressed as civilians') which are trained for more specific internal incidents when there is a risk of chaos spreading all over the country. In May 2003 some 130 reformist lawmakers called on the supreme spiritual leader, Ayatollah Seyyed Ali Khamenei, to accept democratic reforms because they saw this as the only way for the ruling establishment to survive. Later, in June and July 2003, when night-time anti-regime demonstrations were about to expand and teenage demonstrators denounced the leader and his anti-democratic policies, both the Basij and Lebas Shakhsiha poured onto the streets of Tehran. Thousands were arrested.[16] The media, the Internet and satellite television from Los Angeles which gave the news were later accused of provoking the uprising. This was to a great extent true, but

---

[15] 'Safavi: volunteer forces ready to counter cultural onslaught', IRNA, 18 Sep. 2000, URL <http://www.payvand.com/news/00/sep/1088.html>.

[16] Amnesty International, 'Thousands of students arrested in Iran', Aug. 2003, URL <http://web.amnesty.org/wire/August2003/Iran>.

the demonstrations also demonstrate the frustration of the younger generation and the way in which they are challenging the system.

VI. The evolution of external threat perceptions

Until the first Gulf War in 1991, most threats for Iran had been old-style territorial concerns or conflicts with neighbouring states. Once war started with US troops in the region, there was a new strategic atmosphere with which Iran did not feel comfortable at all, but with the withdrawal of Iraqi troops from Kuwait the situation returned to normal. After 11 September 2001 the situation changed again, to the detriment of Iran, and for the first time Iran realized how it had been encircled by foreign troops.

This new environment brought about a revised set of security policy objectives. They included: (*a*) preventing war and contributing to the stability of the region as part of war-torn Iran's move towards development and reconstruction; (*b*) defending Iran's territory and interests on land, at sea and in the air against any external intrusion and attack; and (*c*) protecting and safeguarding Islamic values and the nation's right to live in freedom (as defined by Islamic law), independence and peace 'without resorting to military operations'.[17]

Militarily, Iran had yet to replace the equipment and weapons it had lost during the years of war with Iraq. Because of Iran's hostility to the Western value system, it was facing immense pressures from the outside world. At the same time internally it was entering a period of increasing economic and social demands from a frustrated young population that was determined to change everything, including the Islamic system. As a result, the declared defence doctrine[18] focused more on Islamic values, independence and a few achievements of the 1979 revolution, while putting disproportionate effort into maintaining people's state of preparedness for a 'Sacred Defence'.[19]

---

[17] Part of the objectives explained here can be understood from the many declarations made by the Iranian authorities. See, e.g., 'Defence minister expounds on Iran's security doctrine', *Syasaterooz*, 18 Feb. 2003, p. 7, URL <http://www.netiran.com/?fn=artd(411)>.

[18] See note 17.

[19] There is an extensive literature on the issue of 'Sacred Defence', much like the Soviet 'Great War' literature, See, e.g., the interview with General Safavi in *Jam-e-Jam*, 10 Oct. 2002, p. 6, available in English in 'Protection of national security depends on cultural and economic preservation', URL <http://www.netiran.com/?fn=artd(2993)>.

Iran faced a dilemma: while it wished to see Saddam Hussein and his regime eliminated, it would not work with the USA towards that goal, fearing that in the process the USA would also become a new 'virtual neighbour'. In the wake of the 11 September 2001 terrorist attacks in the USA, Iran could not prevent what it has always tried to avoid—a strong US military presence in the Gulf. In addition to the US and NATO forces on its eastern border with Afghanistan, US and British forces had landed on Iran's western borders for an indefinite period of time.

VII. A strategy of active neutrality

While the US wars on Afghanistan and Iraq eliminated Iran's two major enemies to its east and west, they also brought Iran to a point where, even without Taliban leader Mullah Mohammad Omar or Saddam Hussein, Iran did not feel secure. It suddenly found the United States, NATO and (virtually) Israel on its very borders. Unable to mend fences with the United States and Europe, in this new security environment, Iran had no option but to adjust its strategy.

Iran developed the strategy of active neutrality on the immediate issue of Iraq. On Afghanistan, while showing a more conciliatory approach towards the US war, Iran tried to be of assistance but with no intention of giving any substantial service. On the issue of Iraq, however, things were different. As a major player in the region whose security was at stake, Iran had to clarify its position on certain aspects of the issue.

First, Iran recognized the existence of a serious problem: Saddam Hussein could have produced WMD, and Iranian officials would have liked to see Iraq comply with international law.

Second, Iran preferred to see a solution that involved the international community rather than military action. Iranian officials were therefore relying in particular on the United Nations as the symbol of internationally accepted legitimacy, as opposed to the United States taking unilateral action. As Foreign Minister Kharrazi pointed out, 'We are against war and we feel that through diplomatic means and through the UN we can solve the issue and force Iraq to give up its weapons of mass destruction'.[20] Many countries in the region held similar views.

Third, concerned that such an action would go against the views of the international community and create a precedent for an attack on itself, Iran declared that it was against a unilateral attack by the United States. Some even drew parallels between the US war and state terrorism. For instance, Friday prayer leader Ayatollah Mohammad Imami Kashani said in his 18 October 2002 sermon, 'The White House says if the Security Council does not approve of a military action against Iraq, America will act on its own. This is but to say that the world is moving toward a fire and terrorists are increasing'.[21]

Finally, Iran has clear interests in the Iraqi Shia majority and has never abandoned its religious duty to support them, even during and after the war with Iraq. It is unrealistic to believe that Iran would give up its influence upon and support for the Shia in Iraq. Moreover, Iran strongly took the view that Iraq's sovereignty should remain intact and that its people should decide their own government. The reasoning behind this stemmed from fears of the emergence of a Kurdish state that could give rise to internal instability in Iran, the creation of a pro-US government in Iraq that would enhance anti-regime sentiments in Iran, and a precedent of military intervention by a superpower that could make Iran itself a future target.

Realizing that war might nevertheless occur, regardless of what Iran might wish, before the end of 2002 the Iranian Ministry of Foreign Affairs declared an official policy of active neutrality, which would work to strengthen Iran's role temporarily, both regionally and internationally. This policy had two main components.

The first component was a proactive effort by Iran to prevent the outbreak of war in the region—however unsuccessful. The goal was more than détente between nations; Iran tried to take the lead in efforts against the war. Iranian officials met their counterparts in other countries to discuss the negative outcomes of an attack, emphasized peaceful diplomacy and highlighted the dangers entailed in a war. Efforts were also made by both the president and the foreign minister on a global level. The second component of active neutrality was Iran's commitment to reject the use of force in the event of an attack.

---

[20] 'Straw completes Mid-East mission', BBC News, 10 Oct. 2002, URL <http://news.bbc.co.uk/2/hi/uk_politics/2315473.stm>.

[21] IRNA, 'Senior Iranian cleric cautions UN over anti-Iraq action', 18 Oct. 2002.

The Iranian defence minister commented: 'We are against a war, but we will not oppose it by force . . . at the same time, we will not seek to profit from the situation Iraq finds itself in, and we will also not cooperate with Iraq'.[22]

The removal of its two enemies on the west and east, Afghanistan and Iraq, did not cost Iran a penny. The two major enemies were removed by the US and Coalition forces and, although Iran was generally concerned about war, it had no interest in assisting these operations. By deciding to support international norms rather than military action, Iran's strategy was purely self-protective. However, it was not total neutrality, as it succeeded in obtaining minor appreciation from the US Administration for its behaviour in the war. The US-led invasion of Iraq brought Iran closer to other states of the region and, because of the unexpected difficulties the US occupation is experiencing, Iran will probably continue to benefit from the current very complex situation. However, this is not a win–win situation for Iran as it brings with it major challenges. These are the subject of the next section.

VIII. The occupation of Iraq and Iran's nuclear policy

Initially, Iran saw the US-led occupation of Iraq in March 2003 as a 'crusader war' against Muslim nations and Islam; others saw it as an imperialistic attempt to control the region's strategic resources of oil and gas. Iranian conservatives saw it as a conspiracy against the Islamic regime. Suddenly, President Khatami's détente in foreign policy shifted towards a more pragmatic plan and the goal of self-preservation and self-protection. More importantly, the US presence in Afghanistan and the occupation of Iraq affected Iran's nuclear programme and the completion of the Shahab-3 missile project.

The period after the occupation of Iraq saw a major shift in Iran's nuclear policy. Much as Pakistan used the Afghanistan crisis as a shield to take giant strides towards its nuclear capability, Iran seized the moment of turmoil in the international system as the most appropriate time to move at full speed towards its nuclear goals.

When Khatami was elected president in 1997, Iran was probably still in search of means and ways to build a nuclear weapon, but because the process would take a long time, and because Iran was

---

[22] Agence France-Presse (AFP), 'Iran promises to keep out of US–Iraq war', 1 Oct. 2002.

vulnerable to a possible pre-emptive attack from Israel or the United States, it had to shift gradually from producing a nuclear weapon to producing fuel for nuclear power plants. At the turn of the century and in the post-Iraq occupation era, Iran faced severe challenges of a different nature. Unable to secure sufficient fissile material and components for a bomb, it decided to follow the longer road to developing a nuclear weapon capability indigenously.

In the 1980s and during the war with Iraq, Iran would have preferred to have direct access to a nuclear weapon, but this was nothing more than wishful thinking. The first 15 years of this approach bore no fruit. In the mid-1990s Iran turned to Russia, hoping that the process of completing the nuclear power reactors at Bushehr would help it to acquire the expertise and technology needed to develop a nuclear weapon capability. The deal was also very attractive to Russia, which was seeking to create a market in the neighbourhood for its nuclear power industry. However, Russia did not wish to jeopardize its fragile relations with the USA, and thus the Iranian nuclear energy plan was only able to move forward slowly.

Somewhat earlier, Iran had begun to purchase nuclear material and sensitive fuel-cycle technology through the black-market network organized by Pakistani nuclear scientist Abdul Qadeer Khan. It secretly bought from the Khan network know-how and used centrifuge equipment for enriching uranium. The secret nature of the project, Iran's inability to secure faster and better equipment, and fear of the US and Israeli military reaction, added to factors such as the US military presence to the east and the west of Iran, compelled the system to move at full speed.

Iran's approach was twofold: first, to complete the Bushehr reactor, which had become a matter of national dignity and pride; and, second, in the longer term, to build up technologies that would eventually help it to produce the capabilities needed to assemble a nuclear weapon in a matter of one month or so in the event of an imminent threat. With regard to the latter approach, the illicit cooperation between Iran and the Khan network seemed to be working well.

Publicly, along the same lines as India and Pakistan, Iran adopted the policy of criticizing the discriminatory nature of the NPT regime. However, unlike India and Pakistan—which, along with Israel, are the only UN member states that have never signed the treaty—Iran had signed and ratified the NPT in 1974. It emphasized that, as a non-nuclear weapon state party to the treaty, it had an 'inalienable right' to develop nuclear energy for peaceful purposes and was legally entitled therefore to produce enriched uranium for use in its nuclear power reactors. It had both material and technological support to do so.

In this way, Iran sought to shift international attention from a probable weapon project to the more viable and feasible, and perhaps even economically superior, product—nuclear energy. Whether Iran admitted it or not, however, the fact is that, seen in the context of concerns about dual-use technology, the development of nuclear energy is a parallel route to acquiring a military nuclear capability.

On the basis of this approach, and also on the grounds that it needed nuclear fuel for over 30 planned nuclear plants, Iran decided to develop a complete nuclear fuel cycle, from mining and processing uranium ore for fabrication into reactor fuel to reprocessing spent fuel and storing waste. This decision appeared to be rational and legitimate, and clearly enjoyed a truly national level of support. It also seemed to be unanimously agreed upon by both reformist and conservative factions within the regime.

Referring to attempts made under President Khatami to build confidence among neighbouring states, Javad Zarif, a senior Iranian expert and Iran's permanent representative to the UN, claims that Iran has no intention to use its military capability against its neighbours. He also agrees that Iran 'does not need nuclear weapons to protect its regional interests' and that many of the concerns are based on Iran's 'power disparities and size'. Moreover, there are moral and religious prohibitions against the use of WMD. In addition, according to Zarif, Iran's 'current state of technological development and military capability' does not allow it to rely on 'deterrence against its adversaries' on an international or regional level.[23]

Such statements, convincing though they may be, are inconsistent with the considerable investment and progress Iran has made in developing ballistic missiles, specifically the Shahab-3 series. Moreover, despite Iran's continued diplomatic insistence on its peaceful intentions, the interpretation is still possible that the goal is to keep Iran as close to a nuclear capability as possible so that a shift from one usage to the other would be possible in a short period of time.

Young Iranian technicians have been trained by both Pakistan and Russia. In 2003 about 400 Iranian technicians trained in Russia were

[23] Zarif, J., 'Iran: US nuclear fears overblown', *Los Angeles Times*, 5 Nov. 2004, p. B13.

to replace the 1000 Russian technicians who were installing the peripheral equipment at the Bushehr plant. Another 300 should by now have finished their training by Russia and started working for Iranian nuclear plants. Some of them were originally educated in European universities and then sent to Russia for more specialized training.[24]

For the most part, activities of this kind were kept hidden and pursued in undisclosed locations. The main reason for going underground must be seen in the hostile environment Iran has made for itself during the past 25 years. When President George W. Bush in his State of the Union Address on 29 January 2002 used the term 'axis of evil' and placed Iran in that axis,[25] Iran for the first time felt that it had probably been over-optimistic and perhaps overestimated the power of the reform movement in Iran to change the US Administration's hostile approach to the country. For a short time there had been a widespread belief that the USA would support President Khatami's reform plan. (The Clinton Administration did indeed try as far as it could to support Khatami's reforms, but Iran's own conservatives made progress almost impossible.) With the USA's new 'Global War on Terrorism' and the military attacks on Afghanistan, however, it became apparent that there was no reason for such optimism and soon many people—including many in Iran—believed that Iran would be the next target.

President Bush's statement, followed by the US-led occupation of Iraq, changed everything in the region and in Iran. Suddenly, Iran found itself in a completely different security environment and felt itself strongly encircled by a powerful adversary that was able to use all the instruments of power, including military means, against it. Furthermore, among the US allies in the region Israel came to seem far more threatening for Iran than it had done before. The origins of this animosity go back to the early days of the Islamic Revolution when Ayatollah Khomeini's slogans, such as 'Israel must be annihilated' or 'The road to Jerusalem passes through Karbala' (in

---

[24] 'Continuing Iran–Russia nuclear cooperation', *Iran Report*, vol. 6, no. 11 (17 Mar. 2003), URL <http://www.globalsecurity.org/wmd/library/news/iran/2003/11-170303.htm>.

[25] Bush's statement placed Iran next to Iraq and North Korea in the category he described as an 'axis of evil' which threatened 'America or our friends and allies with weapons of mass destruction . . . Iran aggressively pursues these weapons and exports terror, while an unelected few repress the Iranian People's hope for freedom . . . States like these, and their terrorist allies, constitute an axis of evil, arming to threaten the peace of the world'. The White House, Office of the Press Secretary, 29 Jan. 2002, text available at URL <http://www.whitehouse.gov/news/releases/2002/01/20020129-11.html>.

Iraq, where the shrine of the first Shia Imam Ali is located), shaped Israel's perception of the threat from Iran. When the US-led coalition attacked Iraq, Israel openly hoped that it might also consider Iran as its next target. When rumours about Iran's attempt to achieve a nuclear capability spread, this also triggered a war of words between Iran and Israel.

So far this war has not gone beyond words, but Iran does feel a real threat from Israel and has been trying (*a*) to minimize the risk of war with Israel and (*b*) to deter it from any pre-emptive attack on the Iranian nuclear facilities. The declared Israeli strategy of threatening to bomb Iran's nuclear installations—irrespective of what the strategy actually applied would be—has made its impact.

Iran finds itself within the range of Israeli missiles and air attacks, and is convinced that Israel would not hesitate to attack Iran's nuclear sites in the same way as it attacked the Osirak reactor in Iraq in 1981. It may also attempt to pressure the US Administration to destroy Iran's nuclear facilities. The most recent planned delivery of US-manufactured 'smart bombs' to Israel increases the already existing concerns about an air raid on Iran's nuclear facilities.[26] As a result, from the very beginning Iran's entire new facilities were kept completely secret. Wherever secrecy was not possible and the installations were very visible—as at Bushehr—Iran took care to maintain good relations with the UN and the IAEA on the continuation of work on the nuclear reactors. In fact, in Bushehr everything was transparent and the IAEA had full access to the sites. It could easily contact the personnel involved in the project and Iran would generally cooperate with the IAEA.

From time to time, meanwhile, Russia slowed down Iran's push for nuclear power by delaying the Bushehr agreement in different ways or by making demands concerning the return of spent fuel and radioactive waste to Russia.[27] Since Bushehr is more than 3300 km from the nearest point in Russia, concerns have been expressed in and outside Iran that the transport of spent fuel will be technically unsafe

---

[26] In Sep. 2004 it was reported that the USA had agreed to sell Israel $319 million worth of air-delivered ordnance, including 500 satellite-guided 'bunker buster' warheads capable of penetrating 4-metre-thick cement walls, plus 2500 1-ton bombs, 1000 half-ton bombs and 500 quarter-ton bombs. 'US to sell "bunker busters" to Israel', *International Herald Tribune*, 22 Sep. 2004, p. 7.

[27] Russia had made the supply of fresh fuel to Bushehr conditional on Iran's agreeing to return all spent fuel to Russia.

and environmentally dangerous, as well as economically non-viable.[28] However, the continuation of such arguments between Iran and Russia ultimately served Iran's interests. While the world thought that Russia was exercising good leverage to slow down Iran's nuclear programme, Iran was expanding its capability elsewhere with the help of the Khan network.

This could have gone to the point of no return, but in August 2002 an opposition group that still has some influence inside Iran—the National Council for Resistance in Iran (Mujahedin Khalgh Organization, MKO)—revealed that Iran was building a previously undeclared uranium enrichment facility in Natanz and a heavy-water production plant near Arak.[29] International pressure increased, and Iran had no option but to stick to its legal interpretation of the NPT. The IAEA soon characterized the Natanz site as 'sophisticated and the culmination of a large, expensive effort'.[30] An immediate reaction was the arrest by the Iranian security services of several 'nuclear spies' whose identities have not yet been revealed.[31]

IX. Uncertainties about Iran's nuclear intentions

It appears that Iran has yet to make a decision about its nuclear policy. Whether this is a reflection of factional politics or a clear decision to follow a policy of ambiguity along the same lines as Israel's is difficult to determine at this point in time. In October 2003, after months of denials and inconclusive inspections by the IAEA, Iran acknowledged that it had enriched small quantities of uranium using imported centrifuge components and conducted plutonium separation

[28] The cargo should transit through Azerbaijan and reach Russia after passing through Chechnya or pass through Turkmenistan and Kazakhstan before entering Russia. It could also be shipped via the Caspian Sea, which would make it even more dangerous.

[29] See, e.g., Albright, D. and Hinderstein, C., 'The Iranian gas centrifuge uranium enrichment plant at Natanz: Drawing from commercial satellite images', Institute for Science and International Security (ISIS), ISIS Issues Brief, 14 Mar. 2003, URL <http://www.isis-online.org/publications/iran/natanz03_02.html>.

[30] Albright and Hinderstein (note 29).

[31] The MKO (Mujahedin Khalgh Organization) was among the first groups accused of spying on Iranian nuclear activities but, according to the Iranian journal *Shargh*, quoting the extreme right-wing newsletter *Ya Lessarat al-Hussein*, at least 2 IAEO experts have also been arrested. In addition, *Shargh* argued that *Ya Lessarat al-Hussein*'s accusations about the multinational oil company Shell were one reason why Shell's activities had been restricted in Iran. See 'Hoviyyat-e Jassoussan Atomi Iran' [The identity of Iran's nuclear spies], *Shargh*, 9 Sep. 2004, p. 1, URL <http://sharghnewspaper.com/830619/iran.htm#s108294>.

experiments without declaring these activities to the IAEA. Earlier, in 2002, it had also acknowledged the existence of its project to construct a heavy-water reactor, which was not a violation of its safeguards agreement with the IAEA.[32] Iran has never admitted committing any major safeguards violations and has repeatedly asserted that its nuclear programme is solely for producing electricity and thus allowed under the NPT. The IAEA has continued its inspections, but has not been able to resolve all the outstanding questions about Iran's compliance with its safeguards agreements or to verify that Iran has no undeclared nuclear materials or activities.

The 2004 EU–Iran suspension agreement

It took another year to reach a breakthrough deal between Iran and the E3 aimed at defusing an international crisis over Iran's alleged nuclear ambitions. Finally, on the basis of the deal signed in Paris, the IAEA reported on 15 November 2004 that Iran had agreed to voluntarily suspend all uranium enrichment and related activities as of 22 November, just in time for an IAEA Board of Governors meeting in Vienna on 25 November. Iran agreed to the moratorium on the condition that the E3 would not support US-led efforts on the IAEA Board to refer the file on Iran to the UN Security Council for possible sanctions.

Controversies around the deal began to mount almost immediately. The deal was thrown into uncertainty soon after when the MKO claimed that in 2001 the 'father of the Pakistani atomic bomb', Abdul Qadeer Khan, had 'delivered weapons grade highly enriched uranium to Iran' and that 'Iran plans to use it to build a nuclear bomb next year'.[33] While the Iranian conservative faction seemed to be com-

---

[32] See chapter 1, section III.

[33] The Pakistani Ministry of Information quotes the following from the daily press on 18 Nov. 2004: 'The father of the Pakistani atomic bomb, Abdul Qadeer Khan, delivered a quantity of weapons grade highly enriched uranium to Iran in 2001, which Iran plans to use to build a nuclear bomb next year, an Iranian opposition group claimed in Vienna Wednesday. A senior official of the National Council of Resistance of Iran, Farid Solemani while addressing a press conference in Vienna said, the Iranians have also received nuclear weapons designs from the Khan black market network. Meanwhile, Pakistan yesterday denied an Iranian opposition claim that chief nuclear scientist Abdul Qadeer Khan had transferred highly enriched uranium to Tehran in 2001'. The comment that follows is also interesting: '"This is a highly exaggerated account. Somebody has let his imagination run wild," a senior government official told AFP'. Pakistani Ministry of Information, 18 Nov. 2004, quoting *Dawn* and *The*

pletely dissatisfied with the deal reached in Paris, Western diplomats stated that Iran was rushing to process feed material for the manufacture of weapons-grade uranium. Finally, Iran came under fresh fire from the United States: the outgoing secretary of state, Colin Powell, stated in November 2004 that 'Washington had information that says they not only have missiles but information that suggests they are working hard about how to put the two together'.[34]

Iranian conservatives were pressing for withdrawal from the NPT, following the precedent set by North Korea's withdrawal in 2003. President Khatami and the reformists supported the Paris deal and did not want to create a hostile environment. The president was trying to solve the problem by approaching the European countries—an attempt that seemed to be working for a while. The European countries, however, decided to follow the US and Israeli policy of asking Iran to stop all sensitive nuclear fuel-cycle activities, including uranium enrichment, since that process can produce HEU suitable for use in a nuclear weapon as well as LEU for use in nuclear power reactors.

In the USA and Europe, several questions arise from the ongoing uncertainties. What can be done about the Iranian nuclear challenge? Can a political solution be worked out? For the time being, given the position taken by President Bush—who does not want to be part of the 'E3' negotiation but at the same time does not rule out the military option—a political solution does not seem feasible in the short run, but it is potentially workable.

Another major question is whether it should be left to the IAEA to find a solution to Iran's proliferation challenge. In trying to answer this question it should be noted that the IAEA has been engaged for the past two years in conducting special inspections to verify that Iran is in compliance with its safeguards agreement. It seems that, given the loopholes in the NPT on the one hand and Iran's apparent desire to be judged as being in compliance with the treaty on the other, the IAEA might have some success in temporarily cooling down the controversy and retarding the process of Iran's mastering the full nuclear fuel cycle. However, it will be unable to bring about a

Nation, URL <http://www.infopak.gov.pk/news/pidnews/pidnews2004/pid_nov18_2004.htm>.

[34] Traynor, I. and Goldenberg, S., 'Fresh suspicion over Iran's nuclear aims', *The Guardian* (Internet edn), 20 Nov. 2004, URL <http://www.guardian.co.uk/international/story/0,,1355504,00.html>.

permanent solution to Iran's proliferation challenge unless Iran decides to give up all it has so far achieved.

There remains, however, a military option—for which there is a precedent in Israel's 1981 air strike against Iraq's nuclear reactor at Osirak—that involves the selective targeting of Iranian nuclear facilities. With regard to this third option several scenarios seem plausible, but for any of them to be chosen there would have to be timely and accurate intelligence on the locations of the Iranian facilities, while in reality the quality and reliability of the information available to Western intelligence services are open to question. The information currently available shows that most existing facilities are surrounded by highly populated areas. For instance, in the 1960s, when Iran's research reactor was installed at the Tehran Nuclear Research Centre (TRNC), it was situated outside Tehran city and far from a population centre. Today it is located almost in the centre of the city and surrounded by heavily populated areas. Even a small nuclear accident at the TNRC, let alone a military strike on it, could have catastrophic results. Moreover, if there were a military strike, in addition to unnecessary human damage which would automatically have a negative impact on US prestige in Iran and beyond, there is no guarantee that all facilities would be destroyed. If one part of the facilities remained intact, military nuclear activities could continue, this time perhaps with far more determination.

Perhaps the best option would be to give Iran a chance to prove its peaceful intentions. Following the 2005 presidential election in Iran, things may change. Already within Iran's Supreme National Security Council the dominant trend of thinking is that 'Iran should not destroy its nuclear capacity out of stubbornness' and that 'people do not want to wage a war for nuclear technology'.[35] Seen from Tehran, the agreement signed in Paris in November 2004 is a test of the regime's capacity to build confidence and prove its peaceful intentions. This can also be the beginning of a public debate on the nuclear issue, which traditionally is little talked about by people other than a few scholars and researchers.[36]

---

[35] [Mousavian, head of Iranian negotiation team and the speaker of NSC], *Aftab Yazd* [Persian daily], 20 Nov 2004, pp. 1–2 (in Farsi). See also [People don't want to fight for nuclear know-how], URL <http://www.aftabyazd.com/HtmlFile/MainArchive.htm> (in Farsi).

[36] See note 35.

X. Conclusions

The policy of active neutrality which Iran chose to guide its relation to the US war on terrorism worked for a short while and partly reduced some of its national and domestic concerns about security. With the expansion of the war on Iraq and consequent developments in Iran, only by playing an active and cooperative role within the international community can Iran address the remaining concerns and ensure that it will itself get appropriate assistance at a global level.

Although the implications of active neutrality are fairly positive for Iran, they will not be long-lasting and cannot completely eliminate the threat of the country's becoming the next military target, or reduce the intense political pressure from the West. With the Taliban gone and Saddam Hussein ousted, Iran is likely to be placed in the spotlight as one of the remaining domestically abusive and internationally uncooperative states of the region. Iran needs as much international support as it can muster. Active neutrality is therefore quite simply insufficient; Iran should look beyond such neutrality as a formula for détente and make an effort to improve its image. This may not mean major democratic reform but it does require further efforts to tone down Iran's harsh foreign policy rhetoric, ease up on domestic issues and respect the basic rights of its own people.

The policy of active neutrality has its limits and cannot restore Iran's status as a regional power. It is difficult to believe that it can reduce the level of animosity between Iran and the USA, which is the unavoidable condition for restoring Iran's regional and international position. All the factions that are currently involved in an extremely dangerous competition for power inside Iran have to consider the possible negative outcomes of Iran's 'encirclement' and the potential increase in pressure arising from the 'war on terrorism'. In the absence of Iraq as Iran's old cold war-era rival, the key issue is to create and maintain a unique position in the region and to gather the highest level of support from the international community; yet this imperative in Iran's foreign policy seems to be currently missing.

Khatami's presidency exposed Iran's frozen foreign relations to some warmth, but the stalemate in the domestic power struggle has eliminated the advantages and benefits of some of the small changes that had occurred in foreign policy. Despite some minor successes, the allegations that Iran is sponsoring terrorism and planning to acquire

WMD have not come to an end. No breakthrough in Iran's isolation has yet been observed, and even the Paris deal with the E3 was immediately attacked by Iran's 'conservative parliamentarians' who are close to the spiritual leader, Ayatollah Khamenei. Ahmad Tavakoli, a member of Parliament and a leading supporter of Iran's nuclear activity who opposes giving up what was described as the use of 'nuclear energy for peaceful purposes', criticized the Paris Agreement. He emphasized Iran's rights within the framework of the NPT, stating that 'It is not up to the Europeans to decide over our nuclear program or grant us the right to pursue nuclear projects but, in line with the [NPT], it is our internationally acknowledged right'.[37] Tavakoli represents a large group of like-minded Iranian radicals. Considering the continuity and consistency of his views, it is clear that the Paris Agreement was not based on consensus among the decision makers. In February 2004 Tavakoli stated: 'The young Iranian scientists have succeeded in mastering nuclear technology. It is the right of our people to use nuclear energy for peaceful purposes'.[38]

There is no doubt that Tavakoli has a point about what Iranians have achieved through dedication and hard work, but he ignores the way in which national interest and international security can interconnect. To preserve its interest, Iran has to make a one-time in-depth revision of its foreign and defence policies rather than resorting to emotion and calling upon people's religious conviction.

There is a case for arguing that the international community should not trust Iran but should seek to engage it in a new web of treaties, agreements and legally-binding commitments that would make the production of a nuclear weapon almost impossible. This could have been a rational choice if Iran had been able to resolve its domestic power struggle and speak with one voice. Unfortunately, this is not currently the case. Whether Iran will have the skill, the ability, the political intention and the desire to sincerely invest time, engage in dialogue, and create official and stable foreign relations with Europe and the USA remains completely unpredictable.

---

[37] Deutsche Presse-Agentur (DPA), 'Iran hardliners attack EU deal', 16 Nov. 2004, URL <http://www.expatica.com/source/site_article.asp?subchannel_id=52&story_id=13982&name =Iran's+conservatives+attack+EU+nuclear+deal>.

[38] AFP, 'Iranian conservatives pledge continued cooperation with UN nuclear watchdog', Spacewar.com, 24 Feb. 2004, URL <http://www.spacewar.com/2004/040224151317. hianea1a.html>.

5. The process of national security decision making in Iran: the signing of the Additional Protocol

*Heidar Ali Balouji**

I. Introduction

Disarmament and non-proliferation have become the central focus of the current interaction between Iran and the international community. Any progress in this interaction is tracked closely by observers both within and outside Iran, and the outcome of such interaction has often proved crucial for decision makers in Iran and elsewhere.

Since participation in disarmament and arms control conventions, almost uniquely among national security issues, involves the expertise and the contributions of all the key national security agencies, they play a central role in coordinating policy making and implementation. This process has often worked well, defining the central issues and helping to forge inter-agency consensus on the directions of policy. However, there are other non-official players that also influence national security decision making in Iran, and their exact roles in this process need to be explained and clarified. Because of their direct and indirect roles, too many observers see the process of national security decision making in Iran as ambiguous, so that questions are raised about the decisions and also the decision makers of Iran.

With respect to national security decision making, like all nations, Iran faces a set of choices—what decisions must be made and who will make them. At a higher level, nations have to decide what principles and style of decision making are appropriate for them and, importantly, what structure will govern the process of national security decision making. These are the main questions this chapter discusses. However, in explaining each of these issues, other sub-questions are raised. In addition, in order to discuss national security decision making in Iran in practical terms, the Iranian Government's decision to sign an Additional Protocol to its safeguards agreement

* The views and analyses presented in this chapter are those of the author and do not necessarily represent the views of any institute or organization.

with the IAEA is examined.[1] This section begins with a brief review of the literature.

The analytical background

A look at the literature indicates that there is plenty of material accusing Iran of continued efforts to obtain nuclear weapons. With the report of the IAEA director general to the IAEA Board of Governors session on 16–19 June 2003,[2] the issue of the 'danger' of nuclear proliferation by Iran was once again high on the agenda of the international mass media, and the pessimistic parts of the report were highlighted. For the past decade not only have Iran's nuclear activities been on the agenda in relations between Russia and the USA,[3] but several strategic studies institutes have also focused especially on this issue.

The publication *Iran's Nuclear Weapons Options: Issues and Analyses* purports to explain the reasons why Iran could decide to pursue the nuclear weapons option and withdraw from the NPT; the utility of nuclear weapons in terms of their applicability to Iran's current security situation; Iran's domestic debate on nuclear weapons; and the technical aspects of Iran's missile programmes and the options and limitations these entail.[4] The main assumption of this report is that Iran has already decided to obtain a nuclear bomb; that this decision is increasingly supported by all the factions not only inside but also outside Iran; that Iran has a clandestine programme to

[1] 'The Additional Protocol (INFCIRC/540) is the key to the IAEA's strengthened safeguards system, which is designed to improve the Agency's capability to detect and deter undeclared nuclear material or activities. The Protocol requires a state to provide the IAEA with broader information covering all aspects of its nuclear fuel cycle-related activities, including research and development and uranium mining. States must also grant the Agency broader access rights to nuclear-related facilities and enable it to use the most advanced verification technologies, including environmental sampling.' International Atomic Energy Agency (IAEA), Division of Public Information, 'IAEA safeguards fact sheet', p. 3, URL <http://www.iaea.org/Publications/Factsheets/English/S1_Safeguards.pdf>.

[2] IAEA, 'Implementation of the NPT safeguards agreement in the Islamic Republic of Iran', Report by the Director General to the IAEA Board of Governors, GOV/2003/40, Vienna, 6 June 2003, URL <http://www.iaea.org/Publications/Documents/Board/2003/gov2003-40.pdf>.

[3] Khlopkov, A., 'Iran's nuclear program in the Russia–US relations', *Yaderny Control*, winter/spring 2003, pp. 55–88 (in English).

[4] Kemp, G. (ed.), *Iran's Nuclear Weapons Options: Issues and Analyses* (Nixon Center: Washington, DC, 1 Oct. 2001), URL <http://www.nixoncenter.org/index.cfm?action=showpage&page=kemp>.

develop a nuclear bomb; that it intends to withdraw from the NPT; and that the final purpose of its missile capability is to deliver WMD against its political rivals at the regional or international level. None of the authors of the report has ever been able to substantiate the allegations against Iran. Nor have the most intrusive on-site inspections in the history of the IAEA verified a grain of truth in the assumptions underpinning such biased literature.

While most of the literature on Iran's nuclear activities is focused on its decision to achieve a nuclear bomb, less has been said or written on the Iranian decision-making circles and the way in which they act and are involved in the decision-making process. The latest report published in the West on this issue is the third report of a project entitled Iran's Security Policy in the Post-Revolutionary Era.[5] It states that religion, nationalism, ethnicity, economics and geopolitics are all important in explaining Iran's goals and tactics in its relationship with the outside world, as are the agendas of key security institutions and the ambitions of their leaders. However, the picture it draws of decision making in Iran is characterized by complexity and apparent chaos and, although it pays attention to Iran's national security concerns and agenda, the relationship between disarmament and national security is discussed less. In the meantime, these reports are all speculative in nature and often even contain factual mistakes.

Two papers on decision making in Iran's foreign policy have been published by Iranian authors.[6] The principal issue they consider is the process and approach of foreign policy decision making in Iran but, since foreign policy issues are as strategically important as security issues, and the related decision-making bodies are almost identical, their papers also provide a fair picture of the performance of Iran's decision makers more broadly. However, a specific account of the performance of the structure in terms of deciding to ratify the relevant disarmament and arms control conventions is still needed.

[5] Byman, D. et al., *Iran's Security Policy in the Post-Revolutionary Era* (RAND Corporation: Santa Monica, Calif., 2001). See URL <http://www.rand.org/publications/MR/MR1320/>.

[6] Roshandel, J., 'Evolution of the decision-making process in Iranian foreign policy (1979–1999)', Working Paper 17–1999, Copenhagen Peace Research Institute (COPRI), URL <http://www.diis.dk/graphics/COPRI_publications/COPRI_publications/publications/workingpapers.htm>; and Maleki, A., 'Decision making in Iran's foreign policy: a heuristic approach' (undated), available on the website of the International Institute for Caspian Studies (Tehran), URL <http://www.caspianstudies.com/article/article-E.htm>.

II. Iran's approaches to arms control and disarmament conventions

In general, the prevailing approaches towards disarmament conventions in Iran can be categorized as follows.

1. *The ideological approach*. This is the approach of the current so-called conservatives and the right wing, including most of the opponents of Iran's participation in disarmament and arms control conventions. For them these conventions are tools in the hands of the imperialists who want to suppress Iran's Islamic Revolution of 1979 and change its regime. According to their arguments these conventions are providing mechanisms for espionage and interference in Iran's domestic affairs, and inspections are made with the aim of discovering and then destroying Iran's military capabilities. To prove their case, they refer in particular to the experience of the 2003 war in Iraq, the pressure from the great powers for the disarming of Iraq, and latterly the toppling of the Baath regime there.

2. *The realistic approach*. A few research institutes and strategic studies centres, and a few professors of international relations in Iran who produce briefing reports and policy papers for the Iranian decision makers, analyse the security and strategic environment of Iran on the basis of a realistic vision of international relations. According to this viewpoint, security is the foremost national interest which states should pursue, and for this there is no choice better than self-reliance. By highlighting the disadvantages of the disarmament conventions for the weaker states, they argue that participation in these conventions cannot meet the needs of national security and that if a country is in need of help it is not rational to expect it from others; instead the country must strengthen itself. That being said, none of these research institutes would argue that Iran should 'go nuclear'.

3. *The institutional approach*. In contrast to the above viewpoints, this approach believes that not only is participation in disarmament conventions desirable for the sake of national security but also that it offers other privileges in terms of technological advances and the international standing of member states. This is the approach of most of the reformists, officials of Disarmament and International Security Department at the Ministry of Foreign Affairs, and some professors of international law.

III. Iran's decisions on nuclear policy

In addition to being a party to all the WMD conventions—the BTWC, the CWC and the NPT—Iran has signed the CTBT and is active in the international disarmament forums as well. It has always sought the strengthening of the relevant disarmament conventions and strongly supported the idea of a WMD-free zone in the Middle East.[7] On 18 December 2003 Iran signed an Additional Protocol to its comprehensive safeguards agreement with the IAEA.[8] The process for ratifying the Additional Protocol is still under way, although it is not clear when the Parliament (the Majlis) will hold a vote on whether or not to approve it. To indicate its good will, however, Iran decided to begin to fulfil the obligations contained in the protocol.[9] 'For most of the last year, signing the Additional Protocol, provisionally applying it prior to its ratification and its ratification were among the most important issues that Iran was called upon to do in order to dispel doubts and promote transparency and confidence in its peaceful nuclear program. Now this is fully in place.'[10]

With respect to the disarmament regime, moreover, Iran has its own expectations and criticisms. According to Article IV of the NPT, Iran expects to obtain technical assistance from state parties and expects the lifting of the current sanctions against it. At the same time it sees no legal justification for the discrimination and the application of double standards that can be observed. 'The Islamic Republic of Iran believes that all provisions of the NPT are of equal importance. Maintaining the balance of the "rights and obligations" enshrined in

---

[7] Zarif, J., [The need for a nuclear-free zone in the Middle East], *Ettela'at*, 23 May 1999 (in Farsi).

[8] IAEA, 'Iran signs Additional Protocol on nuclear safeguards', IAEA News Centre, 18 Dec. 2003, URL <http://www.iaea.org/NewsCenter/News/2003/iranap20031218.html>. Iran concluded a safeguards agreement with the IAEA (INFCIRC/214) on 13 Dec. 1974: see URL <http://www.iaea.org/Publications/Documents/Infcircs/Others/infcirc214.pdf>.

[9] IAEA, 'Statement on the implementation of the NPT safeguards agreement in the Islamic Republic of Iran by Director-General for International Political Affairs, Foreign Ministry of the Islamic Republic of Iran Mr Amir H. Zamaninia,', IAEA Board of Governors, 13 Mar. 2004, URL <http://www.iaea.org/NewsCenter/Statements/Misc/2004/zamaninia13032004.html>.

[10] IAEA (note 9).

the treaty, preserves its integrity, enhances its credibility and encourages both universality of NPT and its full implementation'.[11]

Iran's rejection of the nuclear weapon option

Iran's signing of the disarmament conventions has been questioned often, but the following reasons have been offered to prove that the nuclear weapon option is not a desirable option for the country.

1. Iran's positions and actions are based on the Islamic point of view according to which any use of WMD is unjustifiable. These weapons are considered destructive and inhumane. Iran has denounced pro-nuclear positions and called on the members of the international community to eliminate WMD completely.[12] In other words, 'Iran considers the acquiring, development and use of nuclear weapons inhumane, immoral, illegal and against its very basic principles. They have no place in Iran's defense doctrine. They neither add to Iran's security nor do they help rid the Middle East of weapons of mass destruction, which is in Iran's supreme interests.'[13]

Iran, as the victim of the most organized use of chemical weapons ever—during the 1980–88 Iraq–Iran War—is strongly opposed to the use of WMD at all.

2. As a developing country, Iran believes that development in the social and economic sectors is very important. Because of its growing population and its many domestic needs, any use of the national budget for unnecessary expenditure would be economically devastating. Iran also has to pay adequate attention to the non-military aspects of national security—economic, social and political. The experience of developing countries such as North Korea, which tried to invest in nuclear weapons while neglecting its economy, demonstrates clearly the catastrophic results of such policies. Experts have estimated that

---

[11] See the official Iranian statement of 6 June 2003 by Ambassador Ali A. Salehi, Iran's representative at the IAEA, URL <http://www.iaea.org/NewsCenter/PressReleases/2003/06JUNEStatementIRAN.pdf>.

[12] Mohammed Javad Zarif, then Iranian deputy foreign minister, in the parliament session for ratification of the CWC, June 1997.

[13] Aghazadeh, R. (Iranian vice-president), 'Iran's nuclear policy (peaceful, transparent, independent)', Speech at IAEA Headquarters, Vienna, 6 May 2003, available on the SIPRI website at URL <http://projects.sipri.se/expcon/iran_iaea0305.htm>.

for developing countries the cost of developing a nuclear bomb would be roughly 10–15 years of regression in development.[14]

Economically, to provide enough capital to develop a nuclear weapon would be a great burden on a developing country. Moreover, the responses of the international community through policies such as sanctions would add to the obstacles on the path of development. India's and Pakistan's nuclear tests in 1998 led to greater insecurity instead of strengthening their nations' security.[15]

3. Iran is closely surrounded by several nuclear powers. Russia in the north, Pakistan in the east, Israel and (recently) the USA, which has forces stationed to the south of Iran, all possess nuclear weapons. Moreover, Turkey, a Western neighbour of Iran, is a member of NATO, and Iraq had strong motivations to attain nuclear status. However, the resolution of the outstanding problems between Iran and its neighbours does not require the possession of WMD. Hypothetically, any Iranian nuclear arsenal would be poor, not usable against weak neighbours, and ineffective against the strong nuclear arsenals of powerful rivals like the USA. Furthermore, any attempt by Iran to acquire nuclear weapons would probably be met by a pre-emptive attack.[16]

4. Progress in the field of disarmament during the past decade brings with it a glimmer of hope that obstacles can be resolved. At the peak of the cold war, because of suspicion and distrust between the superpowers, issues of inspection and disarmament were not seriously considered. Today, however, thanks to the change in international relations, confidence-building, détente and agreements on disarmament and arms control are an ongoing process and a reality. Hope for total nuclear disarmament exists. Moreover, with the rapid development of technology, which can ultimately change the rules of the game in international relations from the importance of 'hardware' to 'software', the status of nuclear weapons has been weakened.[17]

5. Finally, an international non-proliferation regime cannot tolerate any crossing of its 'red lines'. Even if a country is not a party to the

[14] Tarzi, A., [Non-proliferation regime], [Negah Military and Strategic Reports and Analyses], vol. 1, no. 7 (June 2000), p. 38 (in Farsi).

[15] Mansoori, R., [It happened in the neighbourhood], *Payam-e Emrouz*, June/July 1998, p. 92 (in Farsi).

[16] Mokhtari, M., [Military security in the light of globalization], *Gofteman-e Amniat-e Melli* [National Security Discourse], vol. 1, no. 2 (2001), p. 94 (in Farsi).

[17] Hojjatzadeh, A. H., [Revolution in military security], *Amniat-e Melli* [National Security Quarterly], vol. 1, no. 1 (autumn 1999), p. 106 (in Farsi).

NPT, because of the statement of the UN Security Council in January 1992, any attempt to obtain WMD would be viewed as being against international peace and security. In such a case, the Security Council would be entitled to respond coercively.[18]

In response to the allegations against it, Iran has repeatedly denied that it has a nuclear weapons programme while defending its decision to invest in nuclear power in order to reduce its oil dependency in the long term:

It has already been accepted that some technical failures like other similar cases in the IAEA, have occurred although in this case it has unjustifiably been politicized. We have worked with the IAEA to rectify these technical failures, but it would not mean that we should give in to unreasonable demands that are discriminatory, selective and go beyond the requirements of non-proliferation in accordance with existing IAEA instruments. The benefits of advanced technologies belong to humanity and no nations must be deprived from utilizing them for peaceful purposes.

Iran has declared on many occasions that it has never pursued a nuclear weapon program and will never do so. Our nuclear program is solely for peaceful purposes and therefore, we have principally no problem with the transparency, including the implementation of the provisions of the Additional Protocol. In this direction, we worked and continue to cooperate with the IAEA to remove all doubts about the peaceful nature of our nuclear program at the earliest possible time. Hopefully, all outstanding issues would be solved if and when the politically motivated propaganda allows that.[19]

According to Iranian officials,

Our prime priority of nuclear program is generation of nuclear electricity. Due to the rapid socio-economic development of Iran during the past three decades . . . The second objective in the nuclear development plan of Iran is the attainment of self-sufficiency in the provision of nuclear fuel. Decision to build different types of nuclear power plants obliges us to work for the

[18] United Nations, Security Council, 'Note by the president', UN document S/23500, 31 Jan. 1992.

[19] Statement by H. E. Mohammad H. Fadaifard, ambassador and deputy permanent representative of the Islamic Republic of Iran to the United Nations, before the First Committee of the General Assembly, 58th Session, New York, 14 Oct. 2003, URL <http://www.un.int/iran/statements/firstcommittee/session58/1.html>. On Iran's nuclear energy programme, see IAEA, 'Islamic Republic of Iran', Country Nuclear Power Profile, 2003, URL <http://www-pub.iaea.org/MTCD/publications/PDF/cnpp2003/CNPP_Webpage/pages/countryprofiles>.

production of different types of nuclear fuels, of course, all under the surveillance of IAEA safeguards.[20]

IV. Who are the decision makers?

To appreciate the role and importance of the decision makers in Iran, a review of the constitution, which enshrines the competences of each of the Iranian security institutions, is helpful. However, this can only help to cast light on the official layer of decision making. To analyse the non-official layer it is better to look at civil society and its active players in Iran. They appear to have been increasingly important in decision making since former President Mohammad Khatami took office after his election in 1997. It should also be emphasized that in Iran, as in many other countries, the decision-making process is a dynamic one: at different times and in different situations the role of one player becomes more important and active than that of others. This is especially true in the context of national security issues. For instance, before Iran accepted the Additional Protocol, some political factions and newspapers criticized the protocol and described its acceptance as a betrayal of Iran's national interests, which made it difficult for the decision makers to achieve a consensus earlier.

Furthermore, Iran's decision-making structure is not a static hierarchy. The constitution does not grant a monopoly of decision making

---

[20] Aghazadeh (note 13). In this speech, the following reasons are given to justify Iran's investment on nuclear technology: 'The Islamic Republic of Iran can not merely rely on the provision of its energy from fossil fuels just on the ground of possession of large fossil resources for the following considerations:

'First, these resources are limited and belong to all subsequent generations and unrestrained use of them is not prudent.

Second, the utilization of these resources in processing industries such as petrochemicals will generate much greater added value.

Third, local use of these resources as fuel will drastically affect our foreign exchange earnings from export of crude oil and natural gas. . . . [T]he continued use of energy in its present form in our country is bound to turn our country into an importer of crude oil and some of its by-products in the coming decades.

Fourth, our government is paying considerable indirect subsidies on local fuel consumption which entails heavy costs for the government in a way that the current pricing mechanism does not even meet the production and distribution costs of these fuel products. And the final and very important consideration is environmental issues which are now of concern to the entire international community . . .

The aforementioned considerations have made the reliance of our country on fossil fuels for energy generation unreasonable and unaffordable and have also made the use of new technologies including the nuclear technology more competitive.'

to one single authority.[21] This means that it is even possible for the initiative for a decision to come from the lower layers of that structure. For example, experts and technocrats can initiate accession to an international treaty. They can consider the 'macro' level of national interests and make recommendations. After these discussions the higher officials will decide .

This section considers the role and competence of all the influential players, official and non-official, in the context of Iran's national security policies and especially the decision on acceding to the disarmament conventions.

The official layer

The leadership. The highest-ranking official is Ayatollah Seyed Ali Khamenei, the supreme leader or Vali-e-Faghih (Jurisprudential Guardianship). Where national security issues are concerned, according to chapter 8 of the constitution, his functions and authorities are: determining the general policies of the system; the supreme command of the armed forces; the power to declare war or peace; and the appointment and dismissal of the chief of the Joint Staffs, the chief commander of the IRGC, the chief commanders of the armed forces, and the chiefs of the police forces.

While all these fields are tied up with national security, it is clear that in ratifying, implementing and even deciding to withdraw from disarmament conventions the leadership is the authority which has the final say and the other authorities should obey this decision.

The executive branch. The second-highest authority is the president. He signs and supervises the implementation of laws passed by the Parliament, signs treaties and other international agreements ratified by the Parliament, and presides over the Supreme National Security Council (SNSC).

The main executive branch authorities involved in the disarmament conventions are the ministers for foreign affairs; defence and logistics of the armed forces; intelligence; mines and industry; health and medical education; and agriculture.

The Atomic Energy Organization of Iran (AEOI) has the main responsibility for the technical aspects of Iran's nuclear activities. All nuclear activities in Iran, including nuclear reactors and the operation of safeguards, are under the auspices of the AEOI. Gholamreza Aghazadeh, the head of the AEOI, is also the vice-president of Iran.

The Supreme National Security Council. The SNSC was established to watch over the Islamic Revolution and safeguard Iran's national interests, sovereignty and territorial integrity. According to Article 177 of the constitution, the responsibilities of the SNSC are: (*a*) to determine the national defence and security policies within the framework of general policies determined by the supreme leader; (*b*) to coordinate political, intelligence, social, cultural and economic activities in relation to general defence and security policies; and (*c*) to exploit the material and non-material resources of the country for facing internal and external threats. In line with its responsibilities, the SNSC has established sub-committees such as the defence sub-committee and the national security sub-committee. They are headed by the president or one of the members of the SNSC appointed by the president.

The members of the SNSC are the heads of the three branches of government (the executive, the legislature and the judiciary); the chief of the Supreme Command Council of the Armed Forces (SCCAF); the official in charge of the Planning and Management Organization; two representatives nominated by the supreme leader; the ministers of foreign affairs, the interior and information (intelligence); a minister concerned with the subject; and the highest authorities of the army and the IRGC. Hassan Rowhani, the current secretary of the SNSC, is appointed by the president and in principle is the main representative of Iran in following up the issue of Iran's nuclear dossier before the IAEA and Iran's chief negotiator in this field.

The Parliament. This is the only legislative body in Iran. Among its powers is approving international treaties, protocols, agreements and contracts. In the Parliament the initial discussions of disarmament conventions are carried out at the Commission for Foreign Policy and National Security. Regarding nuclear disarmament conventions, the Commission for Energy is another forum where the technical issues are considered.

The Expediency Discernment Council of the System. Composed of the heads of the three branches of government, the clerical members of the Council of Guardians, and members appointed by the supreme leader, the Expediency Council advises the leader on matters of national policy. Its current head is Hojjatol Eslam Hashemi Rafsanjani.

The Council of Guardians. Composed of six experts in juris-prudence appointed by the supreme leader and six lay jurists who are nominated by the head of the judiciary and approved by the Parliament, the Council of Guardians reviews all legislation passed by the Parliament for its adherence to Islamic law and the principles of the constitution. Ayatollah Ahmad Jannati is its current secretary.

The military. The army and the IRGC are responsible for defending the country and the Islamic Revolution against their enemies. They are not supposed to take sides in politics. The SCCAF represents the views of both of these forces. Regarding disarmament conventions, military advisers participate in the decision-making process by providing advice to policy makers. The latter shape the policies of the country vis-à-vis arms control treaties on the basis of inputs from relevant government agencies, including the army.

The non-official layer

As mentioned above, official decision making is not an isolated process. There is feedback from civil society and civil society activists as well. The more important the decisions, the more intensive the reaction from civil society. Public opinion in Iran seriously follows up issues such as the national position on disarmament. Akbar A'lami, representative of the people of Tabriz and member of the National Security and Foreign Policy Committee in the sixth Majlis, who was also elected to the seventh Majlis, announced recently that an Iranian national movement had been established to defend and support the legitimate and legal rights of Iran in the field of nuclear issues.[22] The results of a public opinion poll conducted by Islamic Republic of Iran Broadcast (IRIB) on 10 November 2004 indicated that 67 per cent of respondents agreed to Iran's pursuing nuclear activities.[23] However, this is rather a dependent variable: in shaping national security decision making, public opinion follows the opinion of the elites.

In recent years, with the new developments in information and com-munication technology, public opinion in Iran has become more aware. Since the end of the cold war there has been a focus on

[22] URL <http://www.baztab.com/news/16703.php> (in Farsi).
[23] URL <http://www.baztab.com/news/17307.php> (in Farsi).

strategic studies and analysis as an area of interest in the research institutes; the volume of publications, including books, journals and monographs, is indicative of the trend. Moreover, to gain an institutionalized insight into strategic issues, not only have the army and other government departments established relevant institutes but even the private sector has shown an interest in this field.[24] The role of the newspapers should also be noted here. They circulate the current news and points of view in relation to national security and disarmament, thus enriching the public debate on such issues. Editorial letters are more effective than they used to be and they reflect the special policy of a particular newspaper and its suggestions to officials.

Needless to say, as in other countries, in Iran political parties, factions and interested groups are demanding more political power to realize their definition of the national interests. They do this by means of announcements, declarations, meetings and demonstrations.

V. How are national security decisions made?

This section reviews the role of each of the above institutions in the process of accepting the Additional Protocol. It does so at five levels of analysis—personal, domestic, national, regional and international.

The personal level

This level of analysis focuses on the role of individual leaders and decision makers. Personal-level analysis can reveal the facts, espe-

---

[24] The Islamic Revolutionary Guards publish: (*a*) [Quarterly on the Iran–Iraq War], URL <http://www.ciw8.net/matter/magazine/negin/negin.asp>; (*b*) [Monthly on Military and Strategic Issues and Analyses], URL <http://www.ciw8.net/matter/magazine/negah/negah.asp>; (*c*) [Specialized Library of War], URL <http://www.ciw8.net>; (*d*) [Quarterly on the History of War], URL <http://www.ciw8.net/Matter/Magazine/M_History_War/HistoryWar.asp>; and (*e*) [National Security Quarterly], URL <http://www.ciw8.net/library/8War_eBook/e Book0030.htm> (all in Farsi). They also have other publications, including the [Quarterly on Military and Geography] and others which appear not to be available on the Internet.

Publications of other research institutes include [Strategic Studies Monthly], published by the Center for Strategic Surveys of the Presidential Office, URL <http://www.css.ir/ bardasht1/no15/> (in Farsi); and the [Strategic Studies Quarterly] (in Farsi), published by the Institute for Strategic Studies, which is affiliated with the Ministry for Higher Education, URL <http://www.risstudies.org/report-f.asp>. The website of the Tehran International Studies and Research Institute, a non-profit institute, is at URL <http://www.tisri.org/ persian.asp> (in Farsi and English). The Imam Hussein University publishes the [Defence Policy Quarterly], URL <http://www.magiran.com/magtoc.asp?mgID =1317> (in Farsi); and the Expediency Council publishes the [Strategy Quarterly], URL <http://www.csr.ir> (in Farsi).

cially in those countries that are dominated by one dictator. Where decisions are made by a single person or limited to a particular instance it can, naturally, be easy to find the 'decision maker'. For example, in Iraq under Saddam Hussein every national decision was Saddam's. However, in most other countries, including Iran, the competence and duties of every authority are prescribed, and no one is authorized to ignore the rule of law. The role of the responsible persons in Iran is therefore considered here through the analyses of the role of institutions.

The domestic level

The socio-political and economic situation of most countries plays a prominent role in shaping important foreign and defence policy decisions. This level of analysis coincides with the non-official layer of influences on decision making described above. In the case of the Additional Protocol, several important domestic factors play an important role and officials have to consider their position and statements on this issue.

Political parties and interest groups are among the domestic players which express their views by means of the available mechanisms. Regarding arms control conventions as a whole, and especially the Additional Protocol before the government signed it, there were two distinct opinions.

On the one hand, the conservatives and the so-called right-wing political parties and interested groups, in criticizing the provisions of the relevant conventions, argued that they were not favourable to Iran's national security and suggested that Iran should not sign the protocol. These political activists organized their protest by means of several demonstrations and continued to question the government's action and protest even after the signing of the protocol.

In the newspapers, reports, articles and letters to the editor published before the IAEA Board of Governors meeting in November 2003 indicated how public opinion was reacting to the issue. Hossein Shariatmadari, the editor of *Kayhan*, a daily newspaper, counselled withdrawal from the NPT altogether on the basis that 'all the sensitive and strategic centres in the country would be open to IAEA inspections and nowhere would be safe any more'.[25] The newspaper later

[25] URL <http://www.kayhannews.ir/830325/2.htm> (in Farsi).

repeated this insistence on withdrawal from the NPT, the resumption of uranium enrichment and refusal to accept inspections according to the Additional Protocol, and suggested to the Parliament that it should not ratify the protocol. *Jomhuriye Eslami* took the same position in an editorial on 22 October 2003, condemning the agreement and the signing of the Additional Protocol as an 'everlasting disgrace'.

The possibility of Iran's signing the protocol led to angry protests in Iran, for example, after Friday prayers on 24 October in Karaj, Qom and Tehran. Students from the Ayatollah Iravani Seminary demonstrated in front of the Ministry of Foreign Affairs in Tehran on 26 October. Yet another protest took place after the 31 October Friday prayers in Tehran.[26]

In its 12 September 2003 resolution, the IAEA Board of Governors requested Iran 'to promptly and unconditionally sign, ratify and fully implement the additional protocol'.[27] The tight and unprecedented deadline (31 October) set in the resolution and its unusual tone and language were criticized by the Iranian public and policy makers alike, and the public anger at the resolution was not merely a blind and emotional reaction: it was based on legitimate questions about the legal authority and accountability of the IAEA, as well as about the fairness of the broader nuclear non-proliferation regime, which have been raised for some time by Iran and some other countries aspiring to develop nuclear energy for peaceful purposes. These questions became particularly relevant after the IAEA Board adopted this harsher approach towards Iran.

1. What level of compliance with arms control treaties by Iran (and perhaps some other states of proliferation concern) will provide sufficient evidence to reassure the US Administration and the EU (e.g., for the resumption of the transfer of technology and materials for peaceful uses of nuclear energy)?

2. What loopholes in the NPT Comprehensive Safeguards Agreements and the Additional Protocol justify the export control regimes and the national restrictions imposed by the members of the Nuclear

[26] Radio Free Europe/Radio Liberty (RFE/RL), 'Iranians exhorted to "arouse US rage"', *Iran Report*, vol. 6, no. 45 (10 Nov. 2003), URL <http://www.rferl.org/reports/iran-report/2003/11/45-101103.asp>.

[27] IAEA, 'Implementation of the NPT Safeguards Agreement in the Islamic Republic of Iran', Resolution adopted by the IAEA Board, GOV/2003/69, Vienna, 12 Sep. 2003, URL <http://www.iaea.org/Publications/ Documents/Board/2003/gov2003-69.pdf>.

Suppliers Group, the Zangger Committee and the US-led Proliferation Security Initiative?[28]

3. The specific powers of the IAEA Board are not defined in the statute of the IAEA. As a result, how can the member states of the IAEA be assured that the Board in its decision making is not playing into the hands of powerful members, thus exceeding its powers by adopting resolutions which are manifestly biased and flawed?

4. How far can the international community rely on the soundness of decisions of a non-accountable body of the IAEA related to non-nuclear weapon states' compliance with their obligations when the major players drafting such decisions are nuclear weapon states (and their NATO allies) who either have not signed the NPT (India, Israel and Pakistan) or have consistently violated it in the past three decades, according to final documents of the NPT review conferences and other documents?

5. What legal (and political) remedies are available to non-nuclear weapon states which are in good standing with respect to their legal obligations vis-à-vis nuclear non-proliferation instruments but are denied their statutory rights under those instruments?

6. To what extent does lack of a common legal language among the member states of the IAEA account for the mishandling of nuclear files by this organization and the prevailing confusion and controversy? Almost every file on a developing country becomes politicized and gets out of the hands of the IAEA, with the result that great powers interfere with that file.

7. What can be done to correct the inherent flaws in the unbalanced provisions of nuclear non-proliferation instruments such as the NPT, the statute of the IAEA, the Model Safeguards Agreement and the Additional Protocol?[29]

The reformists, on the other hand, considering the dangers of not accepting the Additional Protocol, recommended signing it. In the

[28] On the Nuclear Suppliers Group, the Zangger Committee and the Proliferation Security Initiative see, e.g., Anthony, I. and Bauer, S., 'Transfer controls', and Ahlström, C., 'The Proliferation Security Initiative: international law aspects of the Statement of Interdiction Principles', *SIPRI Yearbook 2005: Armaments, Disarmament and International Security* (Oxford University Press: Oxford, 2005), pp. 699–719 and 741–65, respectively.

[29] The questions were originally formulated in an unpublished paper prepared by Dr Behrouz Moradi, Senior Officer at the Legal Affairs Department of the Iranian Ministry of Foreign Affairs, for the SIPRI–Institute for Political and International Studies (IPIS) round table meeting in Stockholm on 4 Mar. 2004. The author gratefully acknowledges his contribution.

meantime they rejected the idea of following North Korea's example and pulling out of the NPT. Some urged signing up to tougher nuclear inspections in order to head off the concerns expressed by the EU, Japan and Russia, as well as the United States. Muhsin Aminzadeh, Iranian deputy foreign minister for Asia–Pacific affairs, stated in an interview that if Iran did not want to build a nuclear bomb—which was the case—then signing the protocol and preserving its civil nuclear capacity was in its interests. Iran must regain international trust by signing the protocol for snap inspections of nuclear sites. It should neutralize the propaganda against its peaceful nuclear activities. If it failed, global public opinion would remain suspicious about its peaceful activities and would block them.[30]

It should be noted that from this time onwards the issue of rejecting or ratifying the Additional Protocol became the foremost foreign policy issue delineating the political factions in Iran. Previously there had been clear differences of policy on several internal political issues, including elections, and the competing viewpoints of the political factions have been highlighted by a few other foreign policy issues, such as Iran's relationship with the USA, the legal regime of the Caspian Sea and more recently a cooperation contract with two Turkish companies; but, compared with the Additional Protocol, they were not enough to delineate clearly the factions' respective positions.[31]

Where public opinion is concerned it should also be recalled that at the first stage, when CNN broadcast pictures of the Iranian nuclear site on 12 December 2002, the attention of the public had not yet been drawn to the Additional Protocol. However, after the CNN coverage and the release of the June 2003 report of the IAEA director general, Iranian society became increasingly sensitive on the issue. The first analyses in the newspapers were not detailed but, after the IAEA Board of Governors decision asked the director general to prepare another report for the October 2003 meeting and requested Iran to sign the protocol, more attention was paid to the issue, and the mass media began to focus on the interpretation of the provisions of the

---

[30] Al Jazeera, News, 23 Sep. 2003, URL <http://www.aljazeerah.info>.

[31] For further detail see Aghai Diba, B., 'Iranian policy in the Caspian Sea: Negotiations, negotiations and more negotiations', Payvand's Iran News, 10 July 2002, URL <http://www.payvand.com/news/02/jul/1000.html>; and 'Iran: Parliament approves to vet Turkish deals', Payvand's Iran News, 26 Sep. 2004, URL <http://www.payvand.com/news/04/sep/1223.html>.

Additional Protocol. Even web loggers took the issue to be important and expressed their views on the protocol.[32]

The campaign for acceptance of the protocol was in part sparked off by socio-economic reasons. For the proponents of the protocol, the increasing needs of the young Iranian society should be met in a proper way and at the right time: they warned that if these needs were neglected Iran would face domestic problems and threats which would be more serious than nuclear proliferation and could put the survival of the system at stake.

The national level

The leadership. In his speeches Supreme Leader Ayatollah Khamenei has emphasized the macro-level policy of Iran. He has spoken of the peaceful purposes of Iranian nuclear technology and the intention of Iran's enemies to deprive the country of this technology, which is a genuine production of Iranian scientists.

A few weeks before the signing of the Additional Protocol, while the debate on its acceptance it was very intense, Ayatollah Khamenei did not involve himself directly in the process, and it was only after the IAEA deadline (31 October 2003) that he went to some lengths, in a speech on 2 November, to assuage Iranians' concerns about the protocol. Permitting the more intrusive inspections which the protocol requires was a way to counter Israeli and US propaganda about Iran's pursuit of a nuclear weapon capability, he stated, adding that this did not mean that Iran would forsake its technological capabilities. He described the Iranian position as a wise measure that did not amount to surrender or to accepting bullying in order to break a conspiracy by the USA and the Zionists against the Islamic Republic.[33]

Thus the leadership did not interfere directly to push forward the acceptance of the protocol. However, all other institutions are accustomed to obeying the instructions and falling into line with the remarks made by the leadership.

---

[32] For further information about the IAEA and Iran as analysed in the Iranian press see URL <http://www.mehrnews.com/fa/NewsDetail.aspx?NewsID=85828> (in Farsi); and URL <http://www.mehrnews.com/fa/Default.aspx?t=Nuclear> (in Farsi). The Mehr News Agency (a private Farsi-language news agency) has allocated a special section on Iran and Nuclear Energy.

[33] URL <http://www.mehrnews.com/fa/NewsDetail.aspx?NewsID=85828> (in Farsi).

The executive branch. President Khatami, several ministries, the AEOI and the SNSC were directly involved in the process of acceptance of the protocol.

President Khatami was the first Iranian official to state publicly that Iranian scientists had succeeded in obtaining nuclear technology. He has insisted on Iran's inalienable right to access peaceful nuclear technology[34] and communicated with the 'E3' powers (France, Germany and the United Kingdom) to encourage them to cooperate with Iran.[35]

The AEOI also played an important role. It had a permanent representation at the IAEA in Vienna.[36] During the negotiations on the Additional Protocol, the AEOI delegation represented the Iranian position on matters related to it. The AEOI also hosts IAEA inspectors and delegations, and handles all issues in dealing with them. It has helped the inspectors to carry out the inspections. However, as is to be expected, its main responsibility remains the technical handling of nuclear activities, and it is conceivable that the AEOI's technical reports have been crucial in briefing other Iranian decision makers and convincing them in adopting a national position on the relevant issues.

The Ministry of Foreign Affairs, as the ministry responsible for diplomacy, was negotiating with other countries and organizations and dispatched several delegations to other countries to clarify the Iranian position on arms control and security issues. Other related ministries covered the aspects of the Additional Protocol that were relevant to them.

The SNSC played the most active role. It has representatives from all related institutions and decides on all issues while taking into account the positions and statements of all the security institutions, so that any SNSC decision indicates a national consensus among all those institutions. As former Foreign Minister Kharrazi stated, it was a deliberate choice of the Iranian system to introduce the SNSC as the main focal point for reflecting the Iranian position on the protocol.[37]

---

[34] See President Khatami's press conference, *Iran*, 1 Feb. 2003, URL <http://www.iran-newspaper.com> (in Farsi).

[35] Mehr News Agency, 'Khatami sends warning letter to EU big three', 14 June 2004, URL <http://www.mehrnews.ir/en/NewsDetail.aspx?NewsID=87012&t=Political> (in English). On the E3 see chapter 3.

[36] This responsibility has recently been transferred to the Ministry of Foreign Affairs.

[37] IAEA, 'Statement by the Iranian Government and visiting EU foreign ministers', Tehran, 21 Oct. 2003, reproduced in appendix A.

The Majlis. During the process of acceptance of the protocol, several members of Parliament (MPs) commented on the issue and a few of the members of the Commission for Foreign Policy and National Security even complained about it: they expected the government to brief MPs in a timely manner and seek the advice of the Majlis in such an important matter. During the sixth Majlis, Akbar A'lami wrote a letter to UN Secretary-General Kofi Annan criticizing the political pressure on Iran to accept the protocol and reiterating Iran's right to have peaceful nuclear technology. This letter was supported by a huge number of other MPs who also signed it.[38]

Before the inauguration of the seventh Majlis on 29 May 2004, some of the newly elected MPs commented on the protocol and warned the IAEA and other countries not to politicize the file on Iran but to adhere instead to the regulations, otherwise they would face problems and make it impossible for the Iranian Government to cooperate smoothly with them. Because of the importance of the protocol, the newly elected MPs established a special committee on the NPT and commented on the issue. At the time of writing, MPs are still commenting on the issue and warning that, if the members of the IAEA Board of Governors make a decision against Iran under US pressure, they can expect the Islamic Republic to adopt a new approach. The decision of the IAEA Board on the Iran dossier would significantly influence the outcome of the Majlis debate on ratifying the Additional Protocol.[39]

The Expediency Council and the Council of Guardians. These two institutions would have a chance to review a Majlis decision on ratification of the Additional Protocol. However, the heads of both issued comments on the question of the protocol and emphasized the importance of peaceful nuclear technology to the country.

The military. The army and the IRGC, as the main institutions for defending national security, also commented on the issue. However, their final position is reflected by the Armed Forces General Staff. In general, they have emphasized their ability and readiness to defend the country and the system against all enemies.

---

[38] 'Letter to Kofi Annan (part 1)', 16 Dec. 2003, text reproduced at URL <http://www.mehrnews.com/en/NewsDetail.aspx?NewsID=45093&t=Political>.

[39] Mehr News Agency, 'Majlis to debate Additional Protocol to NPT after IAEA Board decision: MP', 13 June 2004, URL <http://www.mehrnews.com/en/NewsDetail.aspx?NewsID=86635&t=Political> (in English).

The regional level

The policies of any country, particularly in the realm of arms control and security, are viewed with great care and concern by its neighbours. Countries react to each other depending on the level of amity or hostility between them. With respect to Iran, which has 15 neighbours in the Middle East, the Caucasus, Russia and Central Asia, this interaction becomes very sophisticated.

By the time Iran accepted the Additional Protocol, its relationship with its neighbours had improved. The situation in Afghanistan and Iraq—former enemies of Iran—has changed tremendously in Iran's favour. Moreover, Iran's policy of détente towards its other Arab neighbours, which had supported Iraq in the war against Iran, improved relations with them. This was also true in relation to its non-Arab neighbours. On the issue of signing the Additional Protocol, therefore, not only there was no pressure from the neighbouring countries on Iran, but they even supported Iran in international meetings and conferences. In the regional organizations such as the Organization of Islamic Countries and the Non-Aligned Movement,[40] Iran's neighbours upheld its right of access to peaceful nuclear technology. The same trend was also seen in the individual positions of those countries regarding Iran's nuclear activities.

At the regional level, however, there remained the long-standing hostile position of Israel against Iran. Israel has threatened to attack Iran's nuclear facilities and has resorted to several mechanisms to increase the international pressure on Iran. However, hostility of this sort is not new to Iran.

The international level

At this level the most important factor was the role of the international organizations—the UN and the IAEA—and the main powers among the EU member countries. The interaction between Iran and those players was crucial in Iran's signing the Additional Protocol.

---

[40] IAEA, 'Statement by the Non-aligned Movement (NAM)', IAEA Board of Governors Meeting, Vienna, 12 Sep. 2003, URL <http://www.iaea.org/NewsCenter/Focus/Iaea Iran/bog12092003_statement-nam.pdf>. See also URL <http://www.mehrnews.com/fa/News Detail.aspx?NewsID=87594&t=Nuclear> (in Farsi).

The reports of the IAEA inspectors, and especially that of the IAEA director general, are the basis of any decision of the Board of Governors on Iran's nuclear activities. Iran decided to cooperate closely with the inspectors and to meet the IAEA's request that it accept the Additional Protocol.

However, the reaction of other great powers was important for Iran. Member states of the Group of Eight industrialized nations (the G8), like the EU, had asked Iran to sign the protocol and observe the NPT regulations.[41] The USA in particular initiated international pressure on Iran in order to impose its intentions on Iran. In the IAEA meetings, US diplomats attempted several times to refer the Iran nuclear file to the Security Council, but the other members of the Board of Governors were not convinced of the US reasoning because the Board had yet to find Iran in non-compliance with its obligations (that is, the commitment not to divert nuclear materials from peaceful uses in furtherance of military objectives). The only things at issue were some reporting failures by Iran in the preceding years (all of which have been rectified by Iran). The USA has also tried to convince other countries, especially Russia, to stop their nuclear cooperation with Iran.[42]

Japan as another member of the G8 made a petroleum contract with Iran conditional on Iran's signing the protocol, and only after Iran signed it did Japan finalize the contract. However, there are reports that in the end, because of US pressure, Japan failed to implement this contract.[43]

With increasing international pressure on Iran, Russia, Iran's main nuclear partner, has frequently requested Iran to sign the protocol and has even threatened to stop its nuclear partnership with Iran if the latter did not accept it.[44]

---

[41] 'Non proliferation of weapons of mass destruction: a G8 declaration, 3 June 2003, URL <http://www.g8.gc.ca/nonprolifdef-en.asp>; and IAEA, 'Statement by European Union', IAEA Board of Governors Meeting, Vienna, 8 Sep. 2003, URL <http://www.iaea.org/NewsCenter/Focus/IaeaIran/bog092003_statement-eu.pdf>.

[42] See, e.g., 'Statement on the implementation of safeguards in the Islamic Republic of Iran by United States Ambassador Kenneth C. Brill', IAEA Board of Governors Meeting, Vienna, 13 Mar. 2004, URL <http://www.iaea.org/NewsCenter/Statements/Misc/2004/brill 13032004.html>.

[43] See URL <http://ostadbabak.persianblog.com> (in Farsi).

[44] 'US, Russia warn Iran over nuclear plans', 28 Sep 2003, URL <http://iafrica.com/news/worldnews/273915.htm>.

Finally, on Iran's initiative, the E3—three member countries of the EU (although not acting on behalf of the EU)—became involved in interaction with Iran on the nuclear issue. Their foreign ministers arrived in Iran on 21 October 2003 for consultations with Iranian leaders on the highly controversial issue of the signing of the Additional Protocol. The visit paved the way for the Tehran Declaration of 21 October 2003 whereby Iran agreed to suspend its uranium enrichment programme 'voluntarily', prepare the ground for signing the protocol, and cooperate with the IAEA in providing unrestricted access for its inspectors to Iran's nuclear sites. A joint statement was issued on the basis of the agreement reached with the three European ministers.[45] This took place a week before the 31 October deadline set by the IAEA for Iran to allay international concerns over its nuclear programme or answer to the UN Security Council expired. The result was satisfactory at the time for both sides. On the one hand, Iran bypassed the international pressure while not surrendering to the threats of the USA. On the other hand, convincing Iran to sign the Additional Protocol and stop its enrichment activities was a success for these countries.

VI. Conclusions

Iran supports comprehensive and total disarmament and has frequently asked the nuclear weapon states to comply with articles IV and VI of the NPT, which emphasize technical assistance in the field of nuclear technology and final nuclear disarmament, respectively. The important features of its position are the following.

Continuity and change are obvious features in Iran's participation in the disarmament conventions. Iran was a party to the NPT during the Shah era. At that time it was an ally of the USA and, since it was the Shah who took the final decisions on defence and foreign policy, the real national interest was not considered. However, after the 1979 Islamic Revolution the political regime was changed completely, and the overall policies and methods of decision making also changed. The new government decided to continue participation in the disarmament conventions and membership of the related international organizations. In the meantime, the decision-making process evolved

---

[45] IAEA (note 38).

and now, for a national decision to be adopted, all the related institutions should participate in the process.

The process of decision making in Iran is now sophisticated and democratized. National security policies have to be adopted in a transparent way. In the process of acceptance of the Additional Protocol, all Iran's nuclear policies and activities, as well as related statements and the dynamics of interaction among the different parties inside Iran, were scrutinized by observers at national, regional and international level. No aspects of this process were hidden and every phase was clear to all.

Participation in the various disarmament conventions is a priority of Iran's foreign policy. The focal point for these conventions is the Ministry of Foreign Affairs. Iran has consistently tried to play an active role in the negotiation of arms control and disarmament treaties, thus contributing to the enhancement of international peace and security. Its having been a victim of WMD has strengthened Iran's conviction in this regard.

Iran is not the only IAEA member state that has failed to report certain peaceful nuclear activities in a timely manner. If the IAEA were to scrutinize the nuclear activities of other member states as it did in Iran, the outcome could be even worse.[46]

There are several reasons why Iran, unintentionally, failed to report certain aspects of its peaceful nuclear programme in the past 18 years. The following, *inter alia*, can be mentioned:

The development and implementation in Iran of a State System for Accounting and Control of Nuclear Materials (SSAC) developed by IAEA, which had begun immediately before the Iranian Revolution of 1979 was subsequently disrupted due to the Revolution; nuclear brain drain and loss of institutional memory after 1979 affected timely reporting of nuclear transactions; Iraq–Iran War of the 1980s had almost overshadowed all other activities of the Government agencies; Israel aerial bombardment of peaceful nuclear reactor of Iraq, etc.[47]

This failure of transparency has now been rectified.

In this context, the prospects for the future are as follows. The international community, and especially the USA and its Western allies,

---

[46] On Iran's views on this see note 11.

[47] Excerpt from the presentation by Behrouz Moradi at the SIPRI–IPIS round table meeting, Stockholm, 4 Mar. 2004 (note 29).

with the aim of changing Iran's behaviour, will continue to force on Iran more cooperation and commitments, that is, ratification of the Additional Protocol and a complete stop to its uranium enrichment activities inside Iran. Iran insists that this latter request is contrary to current international law and that any pressure to deprive it of its enrichment facilities under the auspices of the IAEA is illegitimate. However, as in the past, Iran will define its interests in cooperating with the international community. The process of ratification of the Additional Protocol is under way. As the speaker of the seventh Majlis, Gholam Ali Haddad Adel, has stated, the Majlis will decide on its ratification taking Iran's national interests into account and external pressures will not affect its decision. However, the increasing pressure on Iran will face a stronger reaction by the Iranian opponents of support for the arms control and disarmament conventions. In the meantime, this external pressure—which is selective in its current application in the Middle East and other developing countries—will at best be less productive than it has been hitherto.

Finally, it should be remembered that to motivate any country to be involved in an integration process—for instance, accession to international arms control instruments—that country should be provided with concrete incentives. With respect to Iran, these incentives could be binding security assurances, the lifting of economic sanctions, and an end to the use of force or the threat of the use of force in international relations.

6. The EU and Iran: towards a new political and security dialogue

Gerrard Quille and Rory Keane

I. Introduction

The European Union and the Islamic Republic of Iran have long been engaged in developing and deepening their relations. Pre-revolutionary Iran was one of the first countries to attract the partnership of what was then the European Economic Community (EEC). In 1992 this relationship deepened further through a process known as the 'critical dialogue'. The critical dialogue, while not always substantive, was more open and ambitious than the United States' 'dual containment' approach to both Iran and Iraq. While many of the EU member states understood the United States' concerns, they judged the US containment policy towards Iran to be unproductive. In the EU's view, dealing with Iran required a more multidimensional approach based on engagement. Thus, the EU designed the so-called critical dialogue, which was meant to engage Iran in a constructive discussion on human rights, support the 'moderate' Iranian politicians, and prevent the further radicalization of the 'conservatives'.

The critical dialogue was a reflection of the EU's commitment to pursue an active human rights policy as a core element of the newly established CFSP. However, the policy was opposed by the United States and the Iranian expatriate opposition, and was often criticized by the European Parliament for failing to highlight human rights abuses in Iran. It is difficult to assess whether the critical dialogue was successful or not. It can certainly be argued that it could have been much more successful if the EU member states had consistently spoken with one voice on Iran. Unfortunately, at times their economic interests outweighed human rights concerns.[1]

---

[1] For a full overview of the critical dialogue see Struwe, M., *The Policy of Critical Dialogue: An Analysis of European Human Rights Policy towards Iran from 1992–1997*, Middle East Paper no. 60 (Centre for Middle East and Islamic Studies, University of Durham: Durham, 1998).

After the election of the reform-minded Mohammad Khatami as president of Iran in 1997, relations with the EU developed under the 'comprehensive dialogue'. Initiated in 1998, this took the form of meetings, held every six months, between the European Council 'troika' and Iran;[2] it also involved cooperation between the European Commission and Iran in the form of working groups on energy, trade and investment, and meetings of experts on refugees and drug trafficking. While the comprehensive dialogue proved useful, it was clear that the lack of a contractual framework limited the development of such cooperation.[3] This led to a European Council request to the European Commission to draw up a framework for a Trade and Co-operation Agreement (TCA) between the EU and Iran. In December 2002 the Commission launched the negotiations on a TCA with Iran, alongside parallel negotiations on political dialogue and counter-terrorism conducted by the Danish EU Presidency.[4]

Because of the Iraq crisis, during 2002–2003 the EU's security policy role, and in particular its involvement with non-proliferation and disarmament issues, was heightened as never before. The Iraq crisis had the effect of profoundly altering the EU's approach to international affairs as it began, perhaps for the first time, to see issues through a security and nuclear non-proliferation lens.[5] This change in the European approach has directly affected the EU's longer-term engagement, dating from 1997, with Iran. In particular it has brought about a hardening of the European position in relation to the existing four key policy discussions with Iran—human rights; the Middle East peace process; terrorism; and non-proliferation. This change is less a direct response to the present nuclear controversy with Iran than a reflection of a new European concern to have a coherent and common security policy after the serious divisions within Europe (as well as between some European countries and the US Administration) over the US-led invasion of Iraq.

---

[2] The 'troika' are the current and incoming holders of the EU Presidency and the High Representative for the CFSP.

[3] See URL <http://europa.eu.int/comm/external_relations/iran/news/ip_01_176.htm>.

[4] European Commission, External Relations Directorate, 'EU–Iran: launch of negotiations on new agreements with Iran', Press release, IP/02/1862, Brussels, 11 Dec. 2002, URL <http://europa.eu.int/comm/external_relations/iran/news/ip02_1862.htm>.

[5] On the origins of the EU strategy on WMD see chapter 3.

Whatever the rationale, so far as cooperation between the EU and Iran is concerned, the relationship is 'on hold' until the controversy over Iran's nuclear activities is resolved. There has also been little movement on the human rights dialogue between the EU and Iran, as Iran is hesitant to move forward in this area, although, on a positive note, the human rights dialogue did reconvene at a meeting in Tehran on 14 June 2004.[6]

II. Iran's encirclement mentality—more real than imagined

Before looking more closely at the political concerns and the non-proliferation question which overshadow relations between the EU and Iran today, it is useful first to understand why Iran appears unwilling to move forward politically and why WMD proliferation has become such a sensitive question both for Europeans and for Iranians. To understand Iran and address questions such as terrorism and WMD, an understanding of Iran's geopolitical concerns is key.

Iran is bordered to the east by a US-aligned government in Afghanistan, to the west by a US-aligned government in Iraq, and to the north by Turkey, a member of NATO which hosts a strong US military presence. In the conservative Iranian mindset, this means that Iran is effectively encircled by the USA. In addition, India, Pakistan (which shares a border with Iran) and Israel have nuclear capabilities, which makes Iran nervous, especially given Israel's close relationship with the USA and Pakistan's newly acquired strategic friendship with the USA. While the idea of a nuclear weapon-free Middle East is at present not feasible, the implementation of a working road map to peace between Israel and the Palestinians would help to alleviate some of Iran's security concerns and should enable it to move its focus away from regional security. For the time being, however, as Iranian Foreign Minister Kamal Kharrazi stated, 'all Iran's neighbours are prioritized when it comes to foreign policy since they are located

---

[6] The Irish ambassador to Iran, representing the Irish Presidency of the EU in Iran, welcomed the reconvening of the dialogue but emphasized that 'Iran must understand that the TCA only represents one side of the equation. The Iranian government must also move forward on the other side of the equation, namely political and human rights concerns, so as to garner a positive relationship with the EU'. Authors' interview with the Irish ambassador to Iran, Thomas O'Bolster, Tehran, 25 May 2004.

in our immediate security zone'.[7] Beyond these concerns, the US Administration's policy of regime change—as the Iranian political leadership views it—compounds the sense of insecurity and encirclement.[8]

Given these perceptions, the best way for the international community to ensure that Iran remains a non-nuclear weapon state in the long term is to promote non-proliferation and regional disarmament in tandem. Without regional disarmament, it will be difficult to prevent Iranian proliferation unless the international community inserts strong and potentially destructive conditions into any agreements. Conditions would be destructive, for example, if they led Iran to conclude that its membership in the NPT had more disadvantages than advantages and to withdraw from the treaty, as North Korea did. Such a course of action would clearly be detrimental to regional security in the whole Gulf region. To prevent this happening, the international community must conduct policies based on carefully administered conditionality; advocate regional disarmament in the Middle East; and make it clear to Iran that abiding by its legally-binding obligations under the NPT will ultimately help it to develop and become part of a multilateral approach that is capable of restraining unilateral action by other states.

III. The variables of religious and national identity

Beyond the obvious geopolitical security concerns, there are also concerns that the security of Iran's religious and national identity is at stake. The religious security question is not substantially related to the clash between Islam and Christendom. (In fact Christianity is acknowledged in Iran as a true religious tradition, and generally speaking Iranians are likely to trust religious nations more than non-religious nations, irrespective of the variant of faith—the Baha'i faith being an exception to this rule.) Rather, the religious insecurity in Iran derives from the fact that the country is partly encircled by Sunni Muslims, while Iran is inhabited mainly by Shiite Muslims. This

---

[7] Kharrazi, K., 'On Iranian foreign policy', 1 May 2002, URL <http://www.mfa.gov.ir/mfa/English/documents/doc1265.htm>.

[8] Authors' interview with a representative of the Iran Centre for Strategic Studies, Tehran, 24 May 2004.

religious difference is conflated with the national identity variable. In the eyes of many Iranians, 'the Arab–Islamic invasion of Iran in the seventh century put a tragic end to Iran's "glorious" pre-Islamic civilization'.[9] Iranian literature and historiography assert that the Iranians are a proud, non-Arab Persian people. In the past Arab nationalism has tended to side against Iran because of Iran's non-Arab identity: the most obvious example of this was the Arab world's siding with Iraq during the 1980–88 Iraq–Iran War. Iran was also at the receiving end of Arab nationalism in the 1950s, when the Egyptian leader, Gamal Abdel Nasser, increased anti-Persian rhetoric in the Arab world by using the term 'Arab Gulf' rather than 'Persian Gulf'.[10] Additionally, in a long-running dispute with the United Arab Emirates (UAE) over the islands of Abu Musa and Lesser and Greater Tunb, which has eased somewhat in the last few years, the member countries of the Gulf Cooperation Council backed the UAE.[11]

One issue, however, which binds Iran and Arab states in the Middle East is the issue of Palestine and Jerusalem. For the Iranian leadership, official support for the Palestinian cause is an ideological stance. There is also strong support from many quarters inside Iran for Hamas and Hezbollah.

While Iran's intransigence regarding questions about its nuclear activities and its lack of principled commitment to completely stamp out the export of terrorism cannot be excused, they can at least be better understood by taking into consideration Iran's encirclement mentality and the complexity of its national identity. The nuclear issue has become an expression of Iran's policy towards the West, a policy based on vagueness, ambiguity and partial compliance. Equally, it has fundamentally shaped the international community's policy towards Iran in recent months. Specifically, the case of Iran has provided a clear platform for the robust pursuit of the EU's Strategy against Proliferation of Weapons of Mass Destruction, adopted in December 2003.[12]

---

[9] Potter, L. and Sick, G. (eds), *Security in the Persian Gulf* (Palgrave: Houndsmills, 2002), p. 240.

[10] Potter and Sick (note 9).

[11] On 22 May 1998, during a visit to the UAE by Iranian Foreign Minister Kharrazi, the 2 sides agreed to use peaceful means to resolve the ongoing dispute.

[12] On the EU strategy see section VII below and chapter 3.

Before looking at the nuclear issue itself, in order to fully understand the difficulties in moving forward on cooperation between the EU and Iran in all sectors from WMD to human rights, the fundamental characteristics of the political structure and personality of Iran should also be understood. Ultimately, the EU will only be able to put into place mechanisms for resolving the nuclear issue by understanding the domestic and regional political context and by taking that context into consideration in the development of its policy. This is the subject of the next section.

IV. The larger political context

Who shapes the political context in Iran?

According to former President Khatami's official adviser, the political structure in Iran resembles a dynastic democracy.[13] However, the limitations on the powers of democratically elected institutions in Iran are arguably shifting the internal pendulum of power closer to dynasty than to democracy. In dealing with Iran, it is imperative that the international community pinpoint the real locus of power as opposed to the public faces of the regime.

An enforced political revolution?

The 1979 Islamic Revolution led by Ayatollah Khomeini has failed to create an organic Islamic and pious society. Rather, what it has created is an enforced, stern 'public' Islamic state on the one side and 'private' disenchantment and disengagement on the other. While public fervour continues as required in the Friday mosques, privately many Iranians—and in particular many young people under 30 years of age, who make up 75 per cent of the population—do not trust their leading political personalities or political Islam.[14] Nor did they truly respect the reformist leader, Khatami, given his failure to make any

---

[13] Authors' interview with M. R. Tajik, director of the Presidential Strategic Studies Centre, Tehran, 24 May 2004.

[14] A very popular Iranian film of 2004, which depicts a cleric as a thief, points satirically to a growing disenchantment with political Islam. The Iranian authorities consequently banned the film.

substantial progress on political reforms since his election in 1997 and the lacklustre results of his economic programme.[15]

The people of Iran seem to be politically tired and economically stretched. Many are therefore disengaging politically, which means that a revolution based solely on 'people-power' mass revolution is unlikely to occur in the next two or three years.[16] Society's disengagement has both created and resulted from a growing sense of scepticism about the ability of the reformist camp to make any real progress. The ineffectiveness of the reformers was clearly displayed during the summer of 2002 when President Khatami pushed for two vital pieces of legislation in order to take power away from the Council of Guardians and put it into the hands of the elected president through the constitution.[17] Although Khatami stated that these two pieces of legislation were necessary in order to enable him to run the country, neither he nor his supporters in Parliament took any action after the Council of Guardians refused to allow them to be adopted into legislation.

In some respects the failed revolution has produced apathy among the citizens, and indeed among some reformist politicians. The post-revolution generation have become uninterested in reform, as daily life existence takes up enough of their energies as it is. Ironically, the decline of revolutionary zeal plays into the hands of the clerics and conservatives, who prefer to preserve intact the current political and economic system that they created after 1979 and which favours their

[15] M. R. Tajik disagrees with this analysis. He believes that President Khatami ushered in a political atmosphere where opposing ideas were tolerated, developed a sense of civil society in Iran and promoted a more open foreign policy. Authors' interview with M. R. Tajik (note 13).

[16] However, should the conservative Parliament elected in 2004 and/or the new president try to undo the social changes accepted by both the previous, reform Parliament and Khatami, there is a possibility of renewed student anger and protests, as seen in the mid- and late 1990s.

[17] 'The bills would have significantly enhanced the constitutional authority of the presidency while stripping the Guardian Council of its ability to disqualify electoral candidates and veto parliamentary decisions.' International Crisis Group, 'Iran: discontent and disarray', *Middle East Briefing*, Amman/Brussels, 15 Oct. 2003, p. 4. The Council of Guardians—made up of 6 clerics and 6 Islamic jurists and headed by the supreme leader, Ayatollah Sayyed Ali Khamenei—rules the country by Islamic theocracy, supposedly on the basis of the interests of the republic. Its sovereign power derives from the 1979 Islamic constitution and it is both unyielding and omnipresent in all parts of the political establishment. In reality the Council of Guardians, using an interpretation of sharia law, controls almost every aspect of political, social and cultural life, together with most economic dimensions, in Iran.

interests. It would appear that the conservatives have no intention of intensifying the Islamic revolution (as advocated by the most ardent religious conservatives), while many reformers, such as former President Khatami, have not been willing to take steps to bring the revolution to an end (as advocated by the most ardent secular reformers). The more energetic and radical reformers, such as the president's brother, Mohammad Reza Khatami, have now also been effectively sidelined by the conservatives after being banned from standing in the February 2004 parliamentary election.

All means that the international community has no choice but to deal with the structures that exist in Iran. It also means that the international community needs to work on a tenacious multi-year approach towards Iran that is designed to support incremental reforms to the current system. Ultimately, it is likely to be a mixture of incremental structural and political reforms affecting the way in which the country is governed, together with economic growth and increased trade, that will put Iran firmly on the road away from dynasty and towards genuine Islamic democracy.

Iranian interest in the Chinese model

Not surprisingly, given that the Council of Guardians disqualified 2400 reformist candidates from standing, the parliamentary election of 20 February 2004 resulted in victory for the conservatives. It appears that the new government, while maintaining a conservative approach to political, religious and cultural matters, would like to develop a more open economy and attract foreign direct investment. There are indications that Iran is moving towards the Chinese model, based on negligible political and social reforms but greater economic openness. 'For the past several years, Iran's hardliners have been intrigued by China, a regime that has successfully balanced authoritarian politics with economic liberalism.'[18] In the light of this change, it is imperative that the EU continue to encourage reforms across the board, including respect for human rights, which will also bring long-term benefits for Iran.[19] As one senior Western diplomat working in Iran

---

[18] Takeyh, R., 'Iran: From reform to revolution', *Survival*, vol. 46, no. 1 (spring 2004), p. 134.

[19] Authors' interview with Bjorn Larsson, Middle East Task Force, EU Policy Unit, Feb. 2004.

reflected, 'An airplane cannot fly on one wing alone. Therefore the international community must focus not only on the economic but also the political issues, if Iran is to become democratically airborne.'[20] Thus, the EU should continue to link progress towards a TCA with the necessary political reforms.

Especially considering that the pragmatic conservatives[21] appear to be moving towards the Chinese model, it is important for the international community to focus on the political context in Iran, notably on nuclear proliferation, human rights and political freedoms. For some time there has been a school of thought which maintains that Iran should not be overly criticized by the international community but instead encouraged. This viewpoint holds that too much direct criticism would play into the hands of hard-line conservatives in Iran by legitimizing their anti-Western stance and weaken the position of the reformers.

However, in the new environment, since the February 2004 parliamentary election and the 2005 presidential election, this argument is no longer as valid. First, the outcome of the elections has already fundamentally weakened the reformers. Second, given the growing alienation from the original religious spirit of the 1979 revolution and the fact that most ordinary Iranians want to live a normal life and are weary of a feigned Islamic revolution being perpetually imposed on them from above, it is unlikely that direct criticism by the West will in future fundamentally play into the hands of the hardline clerics.[22] What has, however, quite evidently played into the hands of the hardliners in Iran is the hawkish policies of the US Administration in Iraq in 2004, and especially the pictures of Iraqi prisoners being abused by US soldiers. It is difficult as yet to judge how much damage the US policies in Iraq have done to the reform movement in Iran, but on an emotional level it appears to have been considerable.

[20] Authors' interview with a senior Western diplomat, Tehran, May 2004.

[21] 'While both hard-line and pragmatic conservatives reject democratic pluralism as the foundation of the state and have readily collaborated to undermine the reformers, they do have different visions regarding the direction of the Islamic Republic and its policies.' Specifically, the pragmatic conservatives are more likely to cooperate with the EU in return for economic benefit. Takeyh (note 18), pp. 134–35. 'For the international community, it may be possible to strike a deal with the pragmatic conservatives.' Authors' interview with Jesper Hostrup, European Commission, principal administrator, Iran Desk, 25 Mar. 2004.

[22] International Crisis Group (note 17), p. 2.

Human rights and fundamental freedoms

As outlined by many human rights groups, the banning of reformist candidates in the February 2004 parliamentary election and the banning of reformist newspapers—*Sharq* and *Yas-e Nau*—before the election signal a worrying situation where freedom of expression is concerned. The importance of the banning of these newspapers cannot be overstated. The print media are the most important media for access to diverse information in Iran, given that the electronic media are tightly regulated by the establishment. The forced closure of these newspapers reflects the lack of an independent judiciary in Iran. According to Human Rights Watch (HRW), 'the judiciary, which should protect basic rights like free expression, has again taken the lead in violating those rights'.[23] In a briefing to the 60th session of the UN Commission on Human Rights on 29 January 2004, HRW pointed out a number of human rights concerns in Iran, including the absence of due judicial process, the lack of freedom of expression, the use of torture and ill-treatment in detention, and discrimination against religious and ethnic minorities, especially for followers of the Baha'i faith and the defenders of Kurdish language rights.[24] It proposed to the UN Commission the re-establishment of a special mechanism to monitor and report on the human rights situation in Iran.

The international community must take human rights questions seriously into consideration when dealing with Iran. The policy of the UN, the EU and the international community at large must be firm and non-negotiable. Specifically, political prisoners must have their rights restored; judicial reform must be prioritized (perhaps even supported by the international community with expertise); freedom of the press must be assured; and mechanisms should be put in place to identify and resolve cases of ethnic and religious discrimination.

---

[23] Human Rights Watch, 'Iran: Reformist newspapers muzzled before election', *Human Rights News*, 19 Feb. 2004, URL <http://hrw.org/english/docs/2004/02/19/iran7571.htm>.

[24] Human Rights Watch, 'Iran: Briefing to the 60th Session of the UN Commission on Human Rights', Jan. 2004, URL <http://hrw.org/english/docs/2004/01/29/iran7129.htm>.

V. The position of the European Union

Iranian officials often speak of the need to create a multipolar world. In practical terms, this means that Iran should develop stronger ties with China, India, Russia and, most importantly, the EU.[25] For its part, the EU would like to develop stronger ties with Iran; however, in order for it to do so certain conditions need to be met. Both the EU and the USA are clearly aware that speaking with one voice where possible and not taking divergent policy approaches vis-à-vis engagement with Iran can best ensure that Iran implements conditionality clauses such as the EU's non-proliferation clause, adopted in November 2003.[26]

At the same time, the EU's approach to Iran clearly is more understanding and flexible than that of the USA, and thus is seen by Iran as offering more potential. From the EU side the human rights situation, the proliferation of nuclear weapons, terrorism and the Arab–Israeli conflict are all questions (called 'concerns') that affect the progress of the negotiations on a TCA with Iran. Of these concerns, non-proliferation is the EU's highest priority, as specified in the Security Strategy adopted by the European Council in 2003.[27] While formal negotiations on a TCA were launched in Brussels in December 2002, the EU insisted that progress depended on Iran's clarifying the scope and aims of its nuclear programme and accounting fully for its fuel-cycle activities through cooperation with the IAEA. This point was emphasized in the Council Conclusions on 9 December 2003, when the Council reiterated 'the EU's readiness to explore ways to develop wider political and economic cooperation with Iran . . . achieved through full international confidence in Iran's adherence to non-proliferation and, in particular, in the peaceful nature of Iran's nuclear programme'.[28]

---

[25] Keane, R. and Downes, M., 'Deconstructing unipolarity and dialogue amongst civilisations', *Iranian Journal of International Affairs*, vol. 12, no. 4 (Dec. 2000), p. 271.

[26] European Union, Council, 'Note from the General Secretariat', 19 Nov. 2003, 14997/03 PESC 690, CODUN 45, CONOP 54. COARM 16+COPR 1, attachment to annex 1, available on the SIPRI website at URL <http://www.sipri.org/contents/expcon/wmd_mainstreaming. pdf>. See chapter 3 and appendix B.

[27] On the European Security Strategy see chapter 3, section II.

[28] European Union, General Affairs and External Relations Council, 'Iran: Council conclusions', 9 Dec. 2003, extracts URL <http://europa.eu.int/comm/external_relations/iran/ intro/gac.htm>.

Significantly, the EU suspended formal talks with Iran on trade and cooperation in June 2003 because of the scale of the concerns about the latter's nuclear fuel-cycle activities. Some players within the EU hoped that the IAEA would be able to resolve all the outstanding safeguards issues with respect to Iran's nuclear programme expeditiously, which might enable the restarting of the TCA talks. These hopes were raised on 21 October 2003, when the foreign ministers of Iran and the 'E3' (France, Germany and the UK) issued a joint declaration in Tehran announcing that Iran agreed to suspend its uranium enrichment programme in exchange for access to advanced European technology.[29] However, the suspension deal subsequently broke down, making it difficult for the EU to move forward with Iran, at least in the short term.[30]

Finally, after months of negotiations and brinkmanship, on 15 November 2004 France, Germany and the UK signed an agreement with Iran on a new suspension deal.[31] Iran undertook, as a 'voluntary confidence-building measure', to continue to extend its previous suspension to include all enrichment-related and reprocessing activities. The suspension would be sustained, under IAEA verification and monitoring, while negotiations proceeded 'on a mutually acceptable agreement on long-term arrangements'.[32] Following the start in January 2005 of working-level talks between Iran, the E3 and Javier Solana, the Commission resumed talks with Iran on a TCA.[33]

The wider context of conditionality

Beyond the non-proliferation question, the human rights question remains central to EU concerns in dealing with Iran. The Council reaffirmed in its Conclusions on 13 October 2003 that the human

[29] IAEA, 'Statement by the Iranian Government and visiting EU foreign ministers', Tehran, 21 Oct. 2003, URL <http://www.iaea.org/NewsCenter/Focus/IaeaIran/statement_iran21102003.shtml>. The statement is reproduced in appendix A.

[30] See chapter 1.

[31] The text of the agreement is published in IAEA, 'Communication dated 26 November 2004 received from the permanent representatives of France, Germany, the Islamic Republic of Iran and the United Kingdom concerning the agreement signed in Paris on 15 November 2004', IAEA document INFCIRC/637, 26 Nov. 2004, URL <http://www.iaea.org/Publications/Documents/Infcircs/2004/infcirc637.pdf>. It is reproduced in appendix A.

[32] IAEA (note 31).

[33] See chapter 1.

rights dialogue with Iran is one of the means by which the EU can work to improve the human rights situation in the country.[34]

Directly related to concern for human rights is the freedom, or lack thereof, of the press in Iran. Regarding the judiciary, while the EU has gone on record in calling for the Iranian Government to speed up the process of judicial reform, which would work in favour of human rights protection, the reality is that the Iranian Government has very little control over the judiciary, as the supreme leader exerts the right to appoint the head of the latter.

Given the progress it believes Iran still needs to make on human rights and other concerns such as terrorism and non-proliferation, the EU has taken a conditionality approach in linking the negotiations on a TCA with advances on these larger political questions. This type of conditionality is most evident in the linkage made by the EU between progress on non-proliferation issues and the expansion of economic ties with Iran. In fact, on 21 July 2003, the Council concluded that 'progress in economic and political relations with Iran should be evaluated in parallel. More intense economic relations can be achieved only if progress is reached in the four areas of concern, namely human rights, terrorism, non-proliferation and the Middle East Peace Process.'[35]

VI. Iran's intentions and the EU's future strategy

Much of the political anxiety in Europe and indeed internationally about Iran relates to concern over Iran's strategic intentions. In this context the debate over whether Iran has a clandestine nuclear weapon programme takes on added significance, since some analysts believe that a nuclear-armed Iran might be inclined to pursue a more aggressive foreign policy. As this chapter illustrates, Iran's political intentions, including its nuclear policy, are based largely on its regional security concerns, and responding to these concerns is made difficult by the fact that in addressing them the EU and the international

---

[34] Extracts are available at European Union, General Affairs and External Relations Council, 'Human rights: Council conclusions', 13 Oct. 2003, URL <http://europa.eu.int/comm/external_relations/iran/intro/gac.htm#iran131003>.

[35] European Union, General Affairs and External Relations Council, 'Iran: Council conclusions', 21 July 2003, extracts available at URL <http://europa.eu.int/comm/external_relations/iran/intro/gac.htm>.

community are forced to deal with a decidedly undemocratic regime. However, the forces of conservative pragmatism in Iran may be the only channel of power with which the international community can do business, given that the reformers have been largely sidelined and in any case have very little real influence or power, while the ultra-conservatives and clerics, symbolized by the supreme leader and the Council of Guardians, will never 'negotiate' with the West, at least not overtly.

While it is necessary for the EU to pursue a conditionality policy, (especially given the IAEA resolutions), the EU should at the same time endeavour to unconditionally support Iran in many other ways. In addition to the offer to support the development of nuclear power for civilian use in Iran, there are many other sectors where the EU should engage, especially with respect to supporting human security and Islamic democratization in Iran. For example, there are well over 2 million Afghan refugees in Iran, who came across the border for safety both before and at the end of the Taliban regime. Iran can ill afford to take care of so many refugees without international assistance, considering the many domestic economic and social problems it faces—unemployment, inflation, drug abuse and drugs trafficking.[36] The EU can also help to create leverage over Iran by taking a strong, apolitical rule-of-law approach in the Arab–Israeli conflict. An impartial EU policy, as symbolized by previous statements by Javier Solana, the EU High Representative for the CFSP—who condemned the extra-judicial killing of Hamas leader Sheikh Ahmed Yassin on 22 March 2004—gives the Arab countries in the Middle East and Iran

---

[36] 'Unemployment and inflation have seriously undermined the standard of living for most Iranians, contributing to widespread bribery and corruption, late marriages (because couples simply cannot afford it), and drug abuse and addiction. An estimated two million Iranians use drugs and heroin injection is believed to be responsible for the rising HIV/AIDS rate among the prison population. . . . Drug trafficking costs Iran more than $2 billion a year, with 3,300 soldiers and police officers killed in attempts to curb drug imports from neighboring Afghanistan, which is responsible for two-thirds of global opium production. Contrary to expectations, the fall of the Taliban in Afghanistan has actually led to higher levels of opium production.' Abootalebi, A., 'Iran's struggle for democracy continues: an evaluation 5 years after the revolution', *Middle East Review of International Affairs*, vol. 8, no. 2 (June 2004), p. 1.

an indication that the EU is a serious and objective player in the Middle East.[37]

Ultimately, to promote more far-reaching security in the Persian Gulf and the 'Greater Middle East', the EU should consider appointing a special representative for Iran unless progress is made in the coming months. It may also wish to consider promoting the institutionalization of cooperation and joint standards between the Gulf states, modelled perhaps on the European Coal and Steel Community (ECSC). It would also greatly facilitate the chances of peace in the region if all international actors advocated a Middle East WMD-free zone, including Israel. Simultaneously, Iran should be strongly encouraged to destroy its long-range missiles, such as the Shahab-3, which with a reported range of 2000 km has the ability to reach not only Israeli but also Southern Europe.[38]

VII. The EU and Iran: developing a dialogue on non-proliferation?

The EU has been making statements and issuing declarations on issues related to preventing the proliferation of WMD since the creation of the CFSP in the early 1990s.[39] However, in 2003 the EU's activities in this issue area underwent a qualitative change when they were made more coherent and attracted more resources. On 13 December 2003 the European Council (where the EU heads of state and government deliberate and decide) adopted the first European Security Strategy.[40] The document is the first in which the senior political leaders of the EU have established a hierarchy of common threats. It lists the potential threat posed by the proliferation of WMD second, after the threat to Europe from mass-impact terrorism. The potential convergence of these threats, where terrorists acquire WMD,

[37] European Union, Council, 'Javier Solana, EU High Representative for the CFSP, condemns killing of Sheikh Yassin', Press release S0076/04, 22 Mar. 2004, URL <http://ue.eu.int/ueDocs/cms_Data/docs/pressdata/EN/Declarations/79544.pdf>.

[38] 'Iran boasts Shahab-3 is in production', *Jane's Missiles and Rockets*, vol. 8, no. 12 (Dec. 2004), p. 2.

[39] The actions taken up to 2001 are surveyed in Anthony, I., 'European Union approaches to arms control, non-proliferation and disarmament', *SIPRI Yearbook 2001: Armaments, Disarmament and International Security* (Oxford University Press: Oxford, 2001), pp. 599–614.

[40] European Union, 'A secure Europe in a better world: European Security Strategy', Brussels, 12 Dec. 2003, URL <http://ue.eu.int/uedocs/cmsUpload/78367.pdf>.

is listed as the most threatening scenario of all from a European perspective. On the same day the European Council also adopted the EU Strategy against Proliferation of Weapons of Mass Destruction (the WMD strategy).[41] That document, which draws on a set of basic principles agreed in June 2003, set out in more detail the approach of the EU to addressing proliferation threats.

Historically, non-proliferation and disarmament issues have been difficult for EU member states to coordinate. This has been manifest in the tension between the EU's Dual-Use Regulation (controlling exports of goods with potential military as well as civilian applications) and the member states' resistance to the European Commission's oversight of the regulation in respect of their national security concerns. On the macro-political level, divisions also exist because some EU member states are members of NATO, while others are not, and because the EU includes two legally recognized nuclear weapon states, France and the UK, while the other member states are non-nuclear weapon states. These issues have, in one way or another, hindered agreement on substantive common positions or statements in international disarmament or non-proliferation forums.[42] Recent events have stimulated efforts to address these challenges more coherently within the EU.

In particular, the EU has decided to formulate an alternative approach to US policy regarding the use of force to address proliferation challenges. Concerned by the latter's increased willingness to bypass the existing multilateral regimes on the grounds that they have failed to deal with proliferating states, such as Iraq and North Korea, the EU instead seeks to address this through a strategy of 'preventive engagement'[43] which is placed firmly in the context of respecting international law and supporting the UN system. In doing so, it also sets out a programme to improve the non-proliferation regimes. Javier

---

[41] The WMD strategy is described in Quille, G. and Pullinger, P., 'The European Union: Seeking common ground for tackling weapons of mass destruction', *Disarmament Diplomacy*, no. 74 (Dec. 2003), URL <http://www.acronym.org.uk/dd/dd74/74europe.htm>. See also Anthony, I., 'Trends in arms control and non-proliferation', *SIPRI Yearbook 2004: Armaments, Disarmament and International Security* (Oxford University Press: Oxford, 2001), pp. 575–601. See also chapter 3.

[42] Quille and Pullinger (note 41).

[43] Solana, J., 'A secure Europe in a better world' [initial draft of the EU Security Strategy: see note 40], Thessaloniki European Council, 20 June 2003, p. 10, URL <http://ue.eu.int/ueDocs/cms_Data/docs/pressdata/EN/reports/76255.pdf>.

Solana has dubbed this new European approach 'effective multi-lateralism', and it is characterized by a new resolve to pursue common security objectives in a framework that emphasizes multilateral institutions (specifically, the UN and regional organizations) and the rule of law (with an emphasis that military force alone cannot resolve security challenges and key threats), and which acknowledges the root causes of these problems.

In essence, the EU recognizes that the threats must be addressed, but puts the use and limits of force into context: 'In contrast to the massive visible threat in the Cold War, none of the new threats is purely military; nor can any be tackled by purely military means. Each requires a mixture of instruments. Proliferation may be contained through export controls and attacked through political, economic and other pressures while the underlying political causes are also tackled.'[44]

In the view of many observers, the decision of the member states to use the EU as a framework for tackling their common concerns about WMD through a range of instruments represents a historic break-through. The result is a visible determination on the part of the European political leaders to pursue their common security concerns through the EU where they can collectively mobilize powerful trade and economic instruments to apply pressure on third states to pursue a cooperative and regional security strategy.

This new political determination to have a common and coherent security policy after the Iraqi crisis is affecting the EU's negotiations with Iran on a TCA. The EU reopened these negotiations in January 2005, after having suspended them for 18 months, but predicated a successful outcome on Iran providing satisfactory guarantees that its nuclear programme is exclusively for peaceful purposes. This determination and insistence on dealing with security matters before trade and economic issues can be seen as part of an increasing effort by the EU to be consistent in its relations with all third states and partners. Security priorities are thus becoming 'mainstreamed' in an effort to improve coherence in the pursuit of EU security objectives. The key to the new EU approach will be its sustainability in the face of a paradox, whereby a hardening of the EU's position on security

---

[44] Solana (note 43), p. 12.

conditionality undermines the important work carried out over recent years under the comprehensive dialogue between the EU and Iran.

VIII. Mainstreaming non-proliferation

Mainstreaming non-proliferation refers to the process whereby the EU's newly identified security objectives, set out in the European Security Strategy, are pursued by applying pressure across the whole range of instruments available to it. In particular, this means that, for the key security challenges such as WMD proliferation, the member states will apply pressure to third states through the EU to respond to their shared concerns. The approach has been developed from the experience with the 10 new EU member states, where the promise of EU membership was the tool for applying pressure for political and economic reform. Before the European Security Strategy and the WMD strategy were formally adopted, in November 2003 the EU adopted a non-proliferation clause to be applied in all agreements with third states. For example, it has been included in the agreements recently negotiated with Albania, Syria and Tajikistan, and it is being prepared for inclusion in agreements with the Gulf Cooperation Council and the Mercado Común del Sur (Common Market of the South, Mercosur), and with the African, Caribbean and Pacific (ACP) states in the Cotonou Agreement.[45]

The non-proliferation clause

The non-proliferation clause, adopted at the External Relations Council meeting on 17 November 2003 and drawn upon during the recent negotiations with Syria, has two main parts. The first is an 'essential element' that must be included in all third-party 'mixed' agreements and specifies that:

The Parties consider that the proliferation of weapons of mass destruction and their means of delivery, both to state and non-state actors, represents one of the most serious threats to international stability and security. The

---

[45] The June 2000 Cotonou Agreement replaced the Lomé Convention, which had provided the structure for trade and cooperation between the European Communities and the ACP countries since 1975. It is valid for 20 years, subject to revision every 5 years. The full text is available at URL <http://europa.eu.int/comm/development/body/cotonou/index_en.htm>.

Parties therefore agree to co-operate and to contribute to countering the proliferation of weapons of mass destruction and their means of delivery through full compliance with and national implementation of their existing obligations under international disarmament and non-proliferation treaties and agreements and other relevant international obligations.[46]

This element of the non-proliferation clause is a declaratory commitment by all parties to non-proliferation policies, but it does not include any verification procedures or actions.

The second part is made of two elements, which entail further commitments by the parties to (*a*) take 'steps to sign, ratify, or accede to, as appropriate, and fully implement all other relevant international instruments', and (*b*) establish 'an effective system of national export controls, controlling the export as well as the transit [of] WMD related . . . goods, including a WMD end-use control on dual use technologies and containing effective sanctions for breaches of export controls'.

The clause states that these two elements 'might be considered as essential on a case by case basis'. They clearly place major demands on the signatories to the agreement. When read in conjunction with the WMD strategy, this part of the clause seems to imply that states accepting such an agreement would receive support, should they wish, from the EU in the implementation of these provisions, including the setting up of export control and end-user licence systems.

The Syrian experience

Following the 1995 Barcelona Declaration, the European Commission has been negotiating with the 27 Euro-Mediterranean partners towards the establishment of a Euro-Mediterranean Free Trade Area (EMFTA) by the target date of 2010. This is pursued through individual Euro-Mediterranean association agreements (EMAAs) with each state.[47]

The EMAA negotiations with Syria began in 1998 and hence predated the non-proliferation clause; however, Syria had shown a willingness to discuss WMD-related issues as part of discussions on

[46] European Union, Council (note 26).

[47] European Commission, External Relations Directorate, 'EU–Syria: conclusion of the negotiations for an Association Agreement', Press release, IP/03/1704, Brussels, 10 Dec. 2003, URL <http://www.europa.eu.int/comm/external_relations/syria/intro/ip03_1704.htm>.

the Middle East under the Barcelona Process. The European Commission had also anticipated the adoption of the non-proliferation clause and, at least from October 2003, had told Syria that it would have to be included in the EMAA. The Syrian negotiations therefore included language on non-proliferation before the EU adopted the clause in November 2003. The negotiations were approaching their conclusion, and in December 2003 the Commission presented the member states with the draft text. The response was mixed: some were unhappy that the language was not close enough to the text of the adopted non-proliferation clause. The Commission negotiators were asked to revise the text and in January 2004 they reached agreement with their Syrian counterparts on a new text. This text was 'closer' to the non-proliferation clause but some member states still felt that it was not close enough. Subsequently, the Commission has maintained contacts with Syria and, under the Irish EU Presidency during the first half of 2004, the Commission focused its efforts on establishing a common position and text. The Syrian Government made it clear that it would not negotiate again on the text of the non-proliferation clause unless it had the whole support of the EU. Up to early June 2004 the situation remained unresolved, with the European side unable to achieve a common position, and the Commission trying to avoid failure and to maintain contacts with the Syrian negotiators and reassure them that when the issue was next discussed there would be a text that could be approved by both sides.[48]

The member states' difficulties in agreeing a text with Syria stemmed basically from the desire of some member states to push beyond the basic statement of the first part (the 'essential element') of the clause and towards the non-essential elements, which included commitments by Syria to accede to two key international arms control and disarmament treaties—the CWC and the BTWC[49]—and to move towards establishing an export control system and end-user licensing system. These member states argued for language in the text on export controls that is very similar to that in the non-essential element of the clause, as well as language on non-proliferation that is based on the 'essential element'.

---

[48] Authors' interviews with the Syrian desk officer in the European Commission and the head of the Unit for WMD, Brussels, May 2004.

[49] Syria signed the BTWC on 14 Apr. 1972 but has not ratified it.

Within the EU machinery, the European Commission worked with the Presidency to get the issue on to the agenda of the Committee of Permanent Representatives to the EU (COREPER) in order to finalize agreement on the text, which would enable the Commission to reactivate negotiations with Syria. After lengthy internal deliberations, agreement was reached on a new text that reportedly respected the principles and ideas of non-proliferation as included in the model clause (including the essential element) while also mentioning the non-essential elements (including export controls and secure transit of goods). Following preliminary agreement on the text in September 2004, the Commission and Syrian negotiators made rapid progress, culminating on 19 October 2004 with the initialling of an EU–Syria association agreement.[50]

The Syrian case is an interesting early example of how the EU, and in particular the European Commission, has moved quickly to include non-proliferation in its relations with third states and parties, as promised in the WMD strategy and specified in the non-proliferation clause. Syria is also a difficult case because of its importance in the Middle East and because it is a country of concern suspected of activities on, in particular, chemical weapons development. This has made some states nervous about not demanding the adoption of a full clause with both elements.

The European Commission is also concerned about the process of applying the clause in future—that is, how to avoid disrupting and even jeopardizing negotiations, as happened with Syria—and about consistency in decisions as to when to expect a full clause (with all elements) and when to be satisfied with the (weaker) essential element. At present there are 'mixed' agreements (political and economic), which require a non-proliferation clause, and 'Community' (economic) agreements that do not require a clause. (The TCA with Iran is a mixed agreement.) It is unclear, however, what should be done when a country of proliferation concern is seeking a Community-only agreement, as recently occurred with Pakistan. In this case a non-proliferation clause was not legally required, and this

---

[50] European Commission, External Relations Directorate, 'EU and Syria mark end of negotiations for an association agreement', Press release, IP/04/1246, Brussels, 19 Oct. 2004, URL <http://www.europa.eu.int/comm/external_relations/syria/intro/ip04_1246.htm>. The agreement must be approved by the Syrian Parliament and the European Council before it enters into force.

fact may have damaged the political force of the EU's message externally when viewed from contexts where the legal niceties and fetishes of the EU are less well understood.

This is a serious issue and its importance has not been lost on some quarters of the EU, including the European Commission. The Commission has discussed it in the context of its inter-service review (an internal consultation process across all the Commission directorates general), looking at lessons learned from early experience with the clause (including with Pakistan, Syria and Tajikistan, and with the ACP states in the Cotonou Agreement). A non-proliferation clause has meanwhile been agreed with Tajikistan, which is a non-nuclear weapon state party to the NPT, even though the negotiations started after those with Syria. Interestingly, the text is not exactly the model clause because the External Relations Commissioner at the time, Chris Patten, sought to have the text as a 'negotiable' part of the process.

Getting the balance right is also an important part of the successful use of the clause, so that conditionality on non-proliferation does not become an obstacle to the objectives of achieving economic or other political agreements. The European Commission's review is a good first response to getting this balance right and should speed up discussions on identifying which states will be subject to the more demanding and which to the weaker clause. Such a discussion needs to be jointly conducted between the member states through the structures of the Council—perhaps most likely in the Committee on Non-proliferation (CONOP, which includes the Commission) and within the relevant parts of the Commission (the Directorate-General (DG) for External Relations) and other relevant DGs and regional or country desks.

The EU is taking seriously the implementation of the non-proliferation clause in all mixed agreements with third states and parties in support of its new security and non-proliferation strategies. The challenge will continue to lie in applying the clause consistently and deciding in advance which states merit the application of the full clause or just the essential element. This will raise questions about the EU's standards in its relations with certain countries and not others. In any event, the issue of non-proliferation is clearly becoming an important conditional element in the EU's external relations. In this respect Iran might take some comfort in knowing that it is not being singled out and that, even without the nuclear controversy of the past year, the issue of the non-proliferation clause would have resurfaced in the future.

IX. Conditional engagement and the future of EU relations with Iran

The EU's broader policy towards the Middle East is evident in its stance on Iran. For example, its Iran policy is closely coordinated with the USA, every effort being made to speak in harmony on related questions. Partly because of the requirement to keep in synchronization with US policy, the EU policy is evidently cautious and conservative, while there is evidence of a clear prioritization of the non-proliferation question.

As things stand currently, the conclusion of a TCA between the EU and Iran is contingent on the nuclear issue being resolved. The specific elements of the EU policy towards Iran can be summarized as *caution*, *conditionality* and *common sense*. For the foreseeable future the EU's policy towards Iran will remain cautious. It will also be strictly tied to conditionality clauses, in addition to political and human rights questions. There is also a strong common-sense factor at play, however. The geopolitical significance of Iran is not lost on EU policy makers, nor is the internal conflict between reformers and hardliners in Iran. Therefore, while strict conditionality applies, the EU may also support Iran in other ways if this is seen to be in the interest of promoting greater regional and global stability or political reform inside Iran.

X. Recommendations

1. The strength of the European approach to security needs to be considered when engaging with partners in key regions of the world. To succeed, the EU approach should incorporate broader horizons where competing European interests and visions can be reconciled. However, while it is important for the success of its policies that the EU be more united and that its approach to global challenges be made credible, coherent and effective, it would be a shame if this happened at the expense of a regional security dialogue in the Middle East and

of undermining the progress made in recent years with critical partners such as Iran under the comprehensive dialogue.

2. It is recognized that the 'carrots' the EU has to offer are few and that it is unwilling to barter with its main carrot, the TCA. Nevertheless, if progress is to be made on the nuclear non-proliferation question, the EU needs to consider seriously what steps are required in order to re-engage on the three other areas of the comprehensive dialogue, with a clear commitment that the TCA discussions can also be developed in parallel. Ultimately, mechanisms that are capable of addressing the WMD issue can only be created by bringing the larger political context into the equation.

3. Ultimately it is likely to be a mixture of incremental structural and political reforms within the Iranian governance process and policy, together with economic and trade growth, that will put Iran firmly on the road to Islamic democracy. The international community therefore needs to work on a multi-year approach in Iran, based on supporting incremental reforms to the system.

4. For the international community today, the pragmatic conservatives in Iran offer the only possible (if improbable) quick link to promoting and realizing a reform agenda in the short term. The first step in this respect will be to build up a personal and trusting relationship with key pragmatic conservative politicians in key positions of power. Without a trusting and personal relationship between diplomats, diplomacy Iranian-style tends to be less than substantive and forthcoming.

5. The international community must take human rights questions seriously into consideration when dealing with Iran. In this respect the policy of the UN, the EU and the international community at large must be unyielding and non-negotiable. Specifically, political prisoners must have their rights restored; judicial reform must be prioritized (and perhaps even supported by the international community with expertise); freedom of the press must be ensured; and mechanisms should be put in place to identify and resolve cases of discrimination.

6. While it is necessary for the EU to pursue a conditionality policy, it should also endeavour to support Iran in many other ways unconditionally. It should not be forgotten that Iran has the right to a peaceful nuclear programme for civilian use as a non-nuclear weapon state party to the NPT. Iran should also be supported by the EU in the

fight against drug trafficking, on environmental security (especially seismic security) and in supporting the Afghan refugees.

7. An impartial EU policy gives the Arab countries in the Middle East as well as Iran an indication that the EU is a serious and objective player in the Middle East. If the EU is seen as objective, Iran is likely to be more forthcoming, as manifested by the 2003 agreement between the EU and Iran.

8. In order to promote security in the Persian Gulf and the 'Greater Middle East', if little progress is made in the coming months on the issue of Iran's determination to enrich uranium, the EU should consider appointing a special representative for Iran. It would also greatly facilitate the chances of peace in the region if all international actors advocated a Middle East nuclear weapon-free zone. Additionally, Iran should be strongly encouraged to destroy its long-range ballistic missiles, such as the Shahab-3. Greater tangible cooperation between the Gulf states should also be encouraged, perhaps through a formal institutional arrangement.

7. Final thoughts on Iran, the EU and the limits of conditionality

Shannon N. Kile

I. Introduction

For the European Union, the Iranian nuclear issue poses an early and important test for the implementation of its Strategy against Proliferation of Weapons of Mass Destruction.[1] Some European leaders have emphasized the importance of resolving the issue, through EU-led diplomacy, for the credibility of a distinctive European approach to addressing WMD proliferation challenges and for demonstrating that Europe is foreign policy actor to be reckoned with on the international scene. For countries such as Iran, non-proliferation has become the main prism through which the wider spectrum of their political, economic and trade relations with the EU is refracted. In this context, one of the goals of this research report was to present a case study examining, from both European perspectives and the perspective of a 'target' country, some of the problems and possibilities inherent in EU efforts to implement a multifunctional strategy to prevent the spread of weapons and materials of mass destruction.[2]

EU soft power and conditionality

As noted in earlier chapters of this volume, the European Council's adoption of the anti-WMD strategy in December 2003 reflected an emergent consensus among member states that the proliferation of weapons and materials of mass destruction posed one of the gravest threats to their security. It also reflected a shared conviction that non-proliferation must be an essential element in the EU's external action,

---

[1] For a description of the origins and contents of the anti-WMD strategy see chapter 3. The full text is available at URL <http://ue.eu.int/uedocs/cmsUpload/st15708.en03.pdf>.

[2] This builds upon SIPRI's work on identifying the EU's special competences and comparative advantages in reducing the risks of WMD proliferation. See, e.g., Anthony, I., *Reducing Threats at the Source: A European Perspective on Cooperative Threat Reduction*, SIPRI Research Report no. 19 (Oxford University Press: Oxford, 2004); and Bailes, A. J. K., 'US and EU strategy concepts: a mirror for partnership and difference?', *International Spectator*, vol. 39, no. 1 (Jan.–Mar. 2004), pp. 19–33.

including in its relations with third countries, as part of the CFSP. With the adoption of the strategy, the member states put into place a framework within which they undertook to collectively address WMD proliferation risks and challenges worldwide, based on common threat assessments, through a joint action plan at the EU level.

One of the novel features of the strategy is its emphasis on using Community instruments in a conditional way, that is, to create incentives and disincentives aimed at influencing the behaviour of other actors in a direction consistent with EU policy goals and priorities. The use of conditionality derives from the EU's traditional preference for so-called 'soft power' tools and the recognition of the indispensable role of such tools in addressing the root causes of security problems. It is a notion that lay at the heart of the decision, taken by the EU General Affairs Council in November 2003, to 'mainstream' non-proliferation policies into the Union's wider relations with third countries and, in particular, to include a non-proliferation clause as an essential element in so-called mixed agreements (i.e., agreements with both political and economic elements) with third countries.[3] A similar approach has been taken in the new European Neighbourhood Policy (ENP), in which the EU holds out the prospect of closer economic, political and security relations with its regional neighbours in exchange for progress on a variety of priority areas, including non-proliferation.[4]

Iranian criticism of conditionality

The EU strategy's emphasis on conditionality has met considerable criticism in Iran. It has been challenged on normative grounds by many Iranian officials and experts, who complain that that the EU approach treats Iran as the object rather than the subject of policy. They argue that it is based on a misperception or misrepresentation of the country that is common among Westerners, namely, that the Islamic Republic is a threat by its very nature and must therefore be

[3] For a description of the content and legal status of the non-proliferation clause see chapter 3. For detail about how the clause has been implemented see chapter 6. The non-proliferation clause is reproduced in appendix B.

[4] The European Neighbourhood Policy, initiated after the EU's enlargement in May 2004, applies to all non-EU participants in the Euro-Mediterranean Partnership, including key actors in the regional proliferation context such as Egypt, Israel and Syria (as well as 6 countries of the former Soviet Union). For a description of the ENP see URL <http://europa.eu.int/comm/world/enp/policy_en.htm>.

contained and confronted. According to Seyed Kazem Sajjadpour, this 'securitized perspective' rests on the ideological premise that Iran after the 1979 revolution is somehow not a 'normal' country and harbours inherently malign intentions.[5] In the view of Sajjadpour and other Iranian analysts, this premise underlies a European approach to Iran which reduces a complex, multidimensional set of relations to the issues of terrorism, human rights and above all nuclear proliferation. They call for a more holistic approach to security—one that combines traditional 'hard' security issues with those related to economic development and human security.

This criticism arguably overlooks an important aspect of the EU strategy, noted earlier by Christer Ahlström in chapter 3: it commits the member states to collectively address root causes of insecurity and the motivations for states to acquire WMD. Among other measures, this involves enhancing EU efforts in the areas of conflict resolution, development assistance, poverty reduction and the promotion of human rights. It also involves strengthening regional dialogues in order to address underlying sources of conflict and instability that might spill over into Europe.

The Iranian criticism of the EU strategy's 'reductionism' under-scores that there are important differences in how Europeans and Iranians think about security and how they define and prioritize their respective threat perceptions. This suggests that it will be difficult to operationalize a comprehensive security dialogue between the two, based on a positive agenda of shared concerns, as long as European threat perceptions and security priorities are not well understood and properly appreciated in Iran, and vice versa. One consequence of this conceptual disjunction is readily apparent in the current Iran–EU talks: Iranians are puzzled as to why Europeans are so concerned about Iran's nuclear programme, while Europeans are puzzled as to why the Iranians do not seem to understand their concerns.

II. The nuclear conundrum

The IAEA is continuing to investigate Iran's compliance with its safeguards obligations. According to Director General Mohamed ElBaradei in early March 2005, several key questions about Iran's past uranium enrichment and plutonium reprocessing activities have

---

[5] See chapter 2.

yet to be answered, and the agency has not been able to come to a judgement about explanations provided by Iran for several other nuclear-related activities.[6] On the whole, however, IAEA nuclear forensics experts have made good progress in uncovering the history of Iran's nuclear programme, sometimes in the face of active Iranian non-cooperation or concealment efforts. Although the agency is not in a position to conclude that there are no undeclared nuclear materials or activities in Iran, it is systematically clearing up, on an issue-by-issue basis, the outstanding safeguards compliance concerns.

Differing European and Iranian objectives

What the IAEA's special inspections process has not done—and indeed, cannot do—is to bring the E3 (France, Germany and the United Kingdom) appreciably closer to their main objective in the ongoing nuclear talks with Iran—namely, to persuade Iran to abandon the parts of its nuclear programme that are of greatest proliferation concern, in particular its plans to build a uranium enrichment facility and a heavy-water research reactor. These facilities are inherently dual-use in nature. In addition to their peaceful purposes, they can be used to produce the fissile material—in the form of either HEU or plutonium—needed for building nuclear weapons. For many outside observers, this raises the troubling prospect that Iran is putting into place the key elements for a nuclear weapon capability under the cover of a civil nuclear energy programme. There is particular concern about Iran's uranium conversion and enrichment programmes, since these are well along the road towards achieving an initial operating capability.

Accordingly, the main task for the E3 in the ongoing negotiations with Iran has been not so much to fully clarify Iran's past nuclear activities as to restrict the scope and nature of its activities in the future. This was evident in the E3's approach in both the October 2003 Tehran Declaration and the November 2004 Paris Agreement.[7] The expectation from the European side was that Iran's temporary, self-imposed moratorium on enrichment-related activities would pave

---

[6] IAEA, 'Safeguards in Iran: IAEA chief stresses need for more transparency', IAEA press briefing, 2 Mar. 2005, URL <http://www.iaea.org/NewsCenter/News/2005/press_briefing 020305.html>.

[7] For descriptions of these agreements see chapter 1; they are reproduced in appendix A.

the way for a more comprehensive and permanent deal: Iran would give up its enrichment programme in return for guarantees that it could import fuel for its nuclear reactors at concessionary prices; it would also receive economic and trade benefits from Europe as well as gain easier access to advanced technology. Underlying this was the consensus view among the E3, supported by the European Council, that Iran's acceptance of a complete and indefinite cessation of all enrichment activities was the only meaningful 'objective guarantee' that its nuclear programme was exclusively for peaceful purposes.[8]

For its part, Iran insists that its plans for a complete nuclear fuel cycle, from mining to processing and enriching uranium and reprocessing plutonium, are intended to give it an independent capability to produce fuel for an expansive nuclear energy programme. It has categorically rejected calls for it to renounce uranium enrichment in favour of nuclear fuel purchased from foreign suppliers, such as Russia, or produced by new multilateral fuel-cycle facilities. Iran argues that it cannot rely on foreign fuel supplies, since these are vulnerable to disruption by outside political pressure. It also maintains that as a non-nuclear weapon state party to the NPT, it has an 'inalienable right', under Article IV of the treaty, to develop materials and technologies for use in a civil nuclear energy programme.

This position enjoys strong support across the political spectrum in Iran, although there remain sharp disagreements over how far down the path towards a nuclear weapon capability the country should go.[9] For many Iranians, the nuclear programme is a symbol of Islamic modernity—of Iran taking its place among other developed, scientifically advanced countries, despite the efforts by the USA to retard its progress.[10] The programme is also a source of genuine national pride, since it is largely the product of an indigenously-trained cadre of young nuclear scientists and engineers who came of age after the 1980–88 war with Iraq. As a result, the nuclear programme has come to be seen as an intimate part of Iran's national identity and sovereignty. This perception helps to account for the contentiousness

---

[8] European Union, Council, 'Presidency conclusions, Brussels European Council, 4/5 November 2004', 14292/04, Brussels 5 Nov. 2004, CONCL 3.

[9] For a discussion of the debates inside Iran over the nuclear programme see Hadian-Jazy, N., 'Iran's nuclear program: contexts and debates', G. Kemp *et al.*, *Iran's Bomb: American and Iranian Perspectives* (Nixon Center: Washington, DC, Mar. 2004), pp. 51–67, URL <http://www.nixoncenter.org/publications/monographs/Iransbomb.pdf>.

[10] Hadian-Jazy (note 9), pp. 60–61.

of the domestic debate over whether Iran should accept intrusive outside inspections, such as those imposed by the Additional Protocol, and other external constraints on the programme's activities.[11]

Iran's insistence that it has a right under the NPT to develop enrichment and other nuclear technologies for peaceful purposes has rallied support in many member states of the Non-Aligned Movement for its nuclear programme. At the 2005 NPT Review Conference, Iranian officials sought to portray demands from the EU and the USA that Iran forgo the development of a uranium enrichment capability as attempts by the Western industrial countries to perpetuate a discriminatory double standard aimed at restricting the transfer of advanced nuclear technology.[12] This is an argument that has resonated in many non-aligned countries, which see little difference between the US and European positions in important multilateral technology supplier arrangements, such as the Nuclear Suppliers Group. To some extent this argument has succeeded in reframing the Iranian nuclear controversy from one about the proliferation of nuclear weapon capabilities to one about the normative basis for technology stewardship and export controls.

III. The limits of conditionality

The question which raises itself is whether the EU's strategy of conditionality—which includes the prospects of closer political and economic ties with Iran but also, if necessary, the threat of sanctions—can induce Iran to renounce the development of sensitive nuclear fuel-cycle technologies. In practical terms, the challenge facing the E3/EU is to offer a sufficiently attractive package of incentives, backed up by the threat of sanctions, that will persuade Iran to choose its relationship with Europe over its nuclear programme.

At first glance, the EU is well placed to be able to influence the Iranian leadership's cost–benefit calculations regarding the country's nuclear programme. In 2004 the EU was Iran's most important trading partner, with 31.5 per cent of the total market share, as well as its

[11] For an analysis of Iran's decision to sign the Additional Protocol see chapter 5.

[12] Statement by H. E. Dr Kamal Kharrazi, Iranian foreign minister, to the Seventh NPT Review Conference, New York, 3 May 2005, URL <http://www.un.org/events/npt2005/statements/npt03iran.pdf>.

largest supplier, accounting for 44 per cent of Iran's total imports. By contrast, Iran ranked 24th among the EU's trading partners in terms of their total trade volume.[13] The EU and its member states are also major contributors to the international institutions which provide development assistance to Iran. In addition, the historical animosities between the Islamic Republic and the United States make rapprochement between them extremely difficult, whereas relations between Europe and Iran are less complicated.

In talks with Iran since the autumn of 2003, the E3 have achieved some positive results. Their efforts defused, at least temporarily, a major international crisis over Iran's nuclear activities. In addition, they were instrumental in persuading Iran to sign the Additional Protocol to its safeguards agreement with the IAEA and to adhere to the Protocol's provisions prior to its ratification by the Majlis (Parliament). This decision may portend a greater commitment by Iran, which has little in the way of an arms control 'culture', to adhering to the norms, legal and regulatory arrangements, and standard practices which collectively comprise the global non-proliferation regime.

However, during the spring of 2005 there were signs that the negotiations between Iran and the E3 in the high-level Steering Committee were approaching breakdown. The two sides made little progress towards reaching a deal on the nuclear issue containing the 'firm guarantees' and 'objective guarantees' called for in the Paris Agreement. Iran vowed to restart operations at its uranium conversion facility near Esfahan, as a first step towards ending its voluntary moratorium on uranium enrichment-related activities. The E3 warned publicly that such a move would leave them with little choice but to join the USA in referring Iran to the UN Security Council for the consideration of possible sanctions. At the same time, there were press reports of divisions emerging between the European partners over whether to allow Iran to retain a limited but significant enrichment capability, to be accompanied by additional transparency and confidence-building measures.[14]

[13] European Commission, 'Bilateral trade issues: Iran', (no date), URL <http://europa.eu.int/comm/trade/issues/bilateral/countries/iran/index_en.htm>. More than 80% of EU imports from Iran are energy-related (mainly oil products), representing 3.9% of total EU imports of energy products. Iran ranks as the 6th largest supplier of energy products to the EU.

[14] Khalaf, R. and Smyth, G., 'Euro trio's relief over Tehran's nuclear offer may prove short-lived', *Financial Times*, 21 Apr. 2005, p. 6.

Challenges in implementing the EU strategy

It would be premature to conclude that a breakdown in the nuclear negotiations would mean that the approach of the E3/EU, based on conditionality, had irremediably failed. However, the experience from the talks so far suggests that there are a number of general challenges facing the EU that have a bearing on whether its anti-WMD strategy can deliver real and sustainable results in addressing proliferation concerns. Many of these derive from the broader challenge, evident in the implementation of the European Security Strategy, of linking the use of various Community instruments drawn from the three main pillars of EU policies.[15] They are all the more vexing because they come at a time when the EU's future architecture and constitutional arrangements have been thrown into uncertainty by two national referendums rejecting the proposed new European Constitution.

Adopting and maintaining common positions

To the extent that differences have emerged in the negotiating positions of the E3, they highlight an inherent challenge in implementing the EU strategy: it requires harmonizing the sometimes diverging preferences and interests of the member states in order to create a coherent, unified approach to dealing with countries and programmes of proliferation concern. This carries the risk that lowest common denominator positions will prevail in deliberations between member states, especially when potentially contentious decisions, such as about imposing sanctions, are involved. In the nuclear negotiations with Iran, this tendency has been evident—at least in the view of Iranian officials—in the inability of the E3 to respond to Iranian proposals other than by repackaging offers already rejected by Iran. A related risk is that differences within Europe could be exploited by outside actors to paralyse the ability of member states to agree common positions and take collective action at an EU level. In the light of these dangers, it is clear that the effective implementation of the EU strategy will require sustained engagement from decision makers at the highest political level.

---

[15] Bailes, A. J. K., *The European Security Strategy: An Evolutionary History*, SIPRI Policy Paper no. 10 (SIPRI: Stockholm, Feb. 2005), pp. 22–28, available at URL <http://www.sipri.org/contents/publications/policy_papers.html>.

Harmonizing priorities and policy goals

A second challenge for the EU is to ensure that the high priority given to combating the spread of WMD does not eclipse other long-standing objectives in the EU's relations with third countries. There is no inherent tension between non-proliferation and other policy goals, such as promoting democracy and human rights; indeed, they can be mutually reinforcing and produce complementary results. In the negotiations with Iran, the E3 have offered to support Iran's application to join the WTO as an incentive for it to eschew the pursuit of sensitive fuel-cycle technologies. While membership in the WTO would facilitate Iran's integration into the global economy, the organization's requirements for transparency and accountability would also advance other important EU policy objectives vis-à-vis Iran, namely, promoting openness and the rule of law and helping to establish basic protections for commerce and citizens. However, there is a risk that the priority given to non-proliferation objectives in the EU's relations with third countries will mean that less attention is given to other concerns. As Gerrard Quille and Rory Keane note in this volume, the human rights dialogue between the EU and Iran has effectively been put on hold until the controversy over Iran's nuclear programme is resolved.[16]

Calibrating incentives

A third challenge lies in convincing countries of proliferation concern that it pays to cooperate with the EU in resolving questions about suspected WMD-related activities. This in turn requires the EU to spell out what tangible benefits that a country can expect to receive in exchange for taking specific steps to assuage concerns about its activities.

In the nuclear talks with Iran, the EU has run into difficulties in calibrating and clarifying the incentives to be offered to Iran in return for showing improved cooperation regarding its nuclear programme. Following the October 2003 Tehran Declaration, there was disagreement among member states over whether some sort of recognition or reward should be given to Iran for agreeing to sign the Additional Protocol and to impose a voluntary moratorium on its uranium enrich-

---

[16] For a description of the EU–Iran 'comprehensive dialogue' and the role of human rights as an element of conditionality in EU policy towards Iran see chapter 6.

ment activities. The dilemma facing the EU was that it did not have many rewards, or 'carrots', at its disposal, other than the 'big carrot' of the TCA.[17] The view of the E3, which was shared by the European Commission, was that if these were to be used effectively they should not be parcelled out on a piecemeal, quid pro quo basis; rather, there first had to be an improvement in the overall situation inside Iran with respect to democratic reforms and human rights, as well as progress toward resolving the nuclear issue. The result was that many Iranians came away disappointed that their decision to sign the Additional Protocol and suspend uranium enrichment activities did not yield the expected benefits in the form of improved trade ties with EU countries and easier access to European technology.

Raising the costs of non-cooperation

At the heart of the EU's policy of conditionality lies a carrot-and-stick approach to addressing proliferation concerns. In the nuclear negotiations with Iran, what is striking about the application of this approach by the E3/EU is that it has involved almost exclusively carrots. Indeed, other than making general threats to refer the Iranian nuclear file to the UN Security Council for possible sanctions, the main 'stick' wielded by the European negotiators has been the withholding of prospective benefits or rewards. To some extent this reflects the EU's focus on deploying soft power, that is, on influencing the actions of other countries through attraction rather than coercion. It also reflects the fact that Iran has been a difficult case for the EU in terms of generating support for imposing sanctions because of the extensive commercial ties that some member states, in particular Austria, Greece and Italy, have with Iran.

The challenge for the EU lies in making tougher and more credible threats to isolate, politically and economically, countries of concern if they do not cooperate in clearing up suspicions about WMD-related activities. In practical terms, this means that the EU institutions and member states must agree on, and be prepared to apply, a calibrated set of sanctions aimed at convincing those countries that the potential costs of moving ahead with suspect activities outweigh the expected benefits. At one end of the spectrum, these could include measures imposed unilaterally by the EU, or example, blocking access to

---

[17] See chapter 6.

advanced or dual-use technologies, freezing financial assets held in Europe and imposing an arms embargoes.[18] At the other end of the spectrum, they could involve, in cooperation with like-minded partners, referring the country in question to the UN Security Council for possible sanctions or even, as a last resort, approving military action under Chapter VII of the UN Charter.

Strengthening cooperation with the USA

It remains an open question whether the EU has at its disposal a sufficient array of carrots and sticks to convince decision makers in countries of proliferation concern to forgo suspected WMD programmes. For the EU, the task of altering cost–benefit calculations in these countries is especially difficult when, as is the case with Iran's nuclear programme, the most sensitive issues of national sovereignty and security, and indeed pride, are at stake.

As a practical matter, this means that the EU must work together with the United States in addressing proliferation 'tough cases', to coordinate their respective approaches. There are clear differences between these approaches in terms of their relative emphases on strengthening international law and multilateral treaties, enhancing verification and inspection mechanisms, implementing sanctions and using military force. However, to the extent that these differences centre on means and modalities, rather than on fundamental goals, there is ample scope for a beneficial transatlantic division of labour in which the EU and the USA contribute their special competences and build on their comparative advantages and 'strategic personalities'.[19]

It is clear that some form of US engagement is crucial for the success of European diplomatic efforts to resolve concerns about Iran's nuclear activities. Although US policy towards Iran has been framed almost exclusively in punitive terms since the 1979 revolution, the USA does have its disposal a number of incentives, such as lifting bilateral economic and trade sanctions or extending security assurances, which are potentially more attractive to Iran than the package of carrots offered by the EU. To date, however, the US Admin-

---

[18] The EU does not currently have an arms embargo in place against Iran, but there is a political agreement among the member states not to sell or transfer to Iran military equipment and technology. This includes dual-use items such as communications systems and avionics.

[19] Spear, J., 'The emergence of a European "strategic personality"', *Arms Control Today*, vol. 33, no. 9 (Nov. 2003), URL <http://www.armscontrol.org/act/2003_11/Spear.asp>.

istration has refused to engage directly with Iran on the nuclear issue, largely because of an ideologically driven concern that this would confer legitimacy on the Islamic regime. The administration has pressed for Iran's nuclear file to be referred to the UN Security Council while giving only reluctant support to the E3's offers of incentives to Iran.

In the light of this situation, some experts have suggested that a more effective transatlantic strategy for dealing with Iran would involve the USA and Europe essentially switching roles: Europe would become the 'bad cop' and the USA the 'good cop', or at least a 'better cop'.[20] The immediate aim would be to change the cost–benefit calculation of the Iranian leadership, so that pursuing a uranium enrichment capability would be viewed as too costly. This strategy would be consistent with calls for the EU and the USA to jointly announce a graduated set series of punitive measures, leading up to and beyond referral to the Security Council, if Iran does not take steps to resolve their concerns about its nuclear programme.[21] These measures would be coordinated and multilateral, thereby overcoming the weaknesses of past and current unilateral US sanctions on Iran.

Mobilizing regional dialogue

The EU strategy emphasizes the importance of addressing the root causes of regional conflicts and insecurity which lie behind many WMD programmes. This is based on the premise that the most effective way to prevent the spread of WMD is for countries to conclude that they no longer need them: the more secure they feel, the more likely they will be to abandon programmes of concern.

To this end, one of the EU strategy's priorities is to mobilize a dialogue with states in regions of particular proliferation concern with the aim of fostering regional security arrangements and regional arms control and disarmament processes. The launching of a dialogue on WMD within the Euro-Mediterranean Partnership was a concrete step toward this goal, although it excluded states in the Gulf that are not

[20] Einhorn, R., 'A transatlantic strategy on Iran's nuclear program', *Washington Quarterly*, vol. 27, no. 4 (autumn 2004), pp. 21–32.

[21] Perkovich, G., 'Changing Iran's nuclear interests', *Policy Outlook*, Carnegie Endowment for International Peace, May 2005, p. 11, URL <http://carnegieendowment.org/files/PO16.perkovich.FINAL2.pdf>. See also Pollack, K., Saban Center, Brookings Institution, *The Persian Puzzle: The Conflict between Iran and America* (Random House: New York, 2004), pp. 412–14.

part of the Barcelona Process.[22] The EU has also supported calls for the creation of a weapons of mass destruction-free zone (WMDFZ) in the 'Greater Middle East'; this zone would include Israel—a de facto nuclear weapon state which remains outside the NPT framework. In the ongoing nuclear negotiations with Iran, the E3 have reportedly raised the idea of developing a 'political framework' within which new regional security and arms control processes could be initiated, including those aimed at creating a Middle East WMDFZ.[23]

IV. Conclusions

At the core of the EU's strategy is a broad, multilateralist approach to preventing the spread of weapons and materials of mass destruction. One important element of this is a commitment to work to implement fully and strengthen the multilateral arms control and disarmament treaties which provide the legal and normative basis for non-proliferation efforts. A second key element is a commitment to addressing the underlying causes of states' seeking to acquire WMD and to promoting stable international and regional security environments, especially in the regions along Europe's periphery.

The Iranian nuclear controversy highlights some of the challenges facing the EU as it attempts to turn the WMD strategy's rhetoric about making multilateralism effective into reality. These include the perennial problems of internal coordination and governance that have weakened the EU as a foreign policy actor. In the light of the current crisis over the proposed EU constitution, it seem likely that in the near term EU policy towards 'tough' cases such as Iran will be shaped largely by a vanguard of individual member states, acting on their own initiative and in their respective national capacities, with the support of the high representative for the CFSP. This will require engagement at the highest political levels in formulating and main-

---

[22] European Commission, 'EU strategic partnership with the Mediterranean and the Middle East: final report', *Euromed Report*, no. 78 (23 June 2004), URL <http://europa.eu. int/comm/external_relations/euromed/publication/2004/euromed_report_78_en.pdf>.

[23] Some experts have suggested that the short-lived Arms Control and Regional Security (ACRS) working group of the Arab–Israeli multilateral peace process, which focused on incremental confidence-building measures to encourage cooperative security norms, provides a useful and instructive precedent for future regional efforts. See Jones, P., 'Arms control in the Middle East: is it time to renew ACRS?', United Nations Institute for Disarmament Research (UNIDIR), *Disarmament Forum*, no. 2 (2005), pp. 55–62.

taining common positions, with the aim of pulling together all the member states in the pursuit of shared objectives.

There must also be more serious consideration of what positive incentives and security measures can be used to persuade states to abandon WMD ambitions. At the same time, the EU and its member states must show a greater willingness to consider imposing sanctions and taking other punitive actions against countries that are suspected of violating important arms control and disarmament treaty commitments or the underlying norms. This in turn means that the EU has to work more closely together with other actors who share its objectives. Among these are, first and foremost, the United States, but they also include Russia, which is key nuclear supplier to Iran, as well as other members of the Group of Eight industrialized countries (the G8) and the IAEA.

Over the near term, it seems likely that Iran will restart operations at its uranium conversion plant and eventually move ahead with a scaled-down uranium enrichment programme. These moves will not necessarily mark the end of discussions between the E3/EU and Iran over the latter's nuclear programme. However, it will be difficult for the E3/EU to continue the current talks with Iran after the latter has crossed an important 'red line' drawn by the EU. What is at stake is the EU's credibility as an external political actor. It will be incumbent on the EU to come together with like-minded partners in agreeing on what steps should be taken to resolve their concerns about Iran's steady progress towards developing a nuclear weapon capability. With the adoption of a common strategy, the EU must be prepared to contribute with unified, hard-headed positions in order to ensure that these next steps are in a direction that is consistent with its multilateralist preferences and convictions.

Appendix A. The agreements between the EU and Iran

The EU–Iran agreement of 21 October 2003 (the Tehran Declaration)

1. Upon the invitation of the Government of the Islamic Republic of Iran the Foreign Ministers of Britain, France and Germany paid a visit to Tehran on October 21, 2003.

The Iranian authorities and the ministers, following extensive consultations, agreed on measures aimed at the settlement of all outstanding IAEA . . . issues with regards to the Iranian nuclear programme and at enhancing confidence for peaceful cooperation in the nuclear field.

2. The Iranian authorities reaffirmed that nuclear weapons have no place in Iran's defence doctrine and that its nuclear programme and activities have been exclusively in the peaceful domain. They reiterated Iran's commitment to the nuclear non-proliferation regime and informed the ministers that:

a. The Iranian Government has decided to engage in full co-operation with the IAEA to address and resolve through full transparency all requirements and outstanding issues of the Agency and clarify and correct any possible failures and deficiencies within the IAEA.

b. To promote confidence with a view to removing existing barriers for co-operation in the nuclear field:

i. having received the necessary clarifications, the Iranian Government has decided to sign the IAEA Additional Protocol and commence ratification procedures. As a confirmation of its good intentions the Iranian Government will continue to co-operate with the Agency in accordance with the Protocol in advance of its ratification.

ii. while Iran has a right within the nuclear non-proliferation regime to develop nuclear energy for peaceful purposes it has decided voluntarily to suspend all uranium enrichment and reprocessing activities as defined by the IAEA.

Dialogue

3. The Foreign Ministers of Britain, France and Germany welcomed the decisions of the Iranian Government and informed the Iranian authorities that:

a. Their governments recognise the right of Iran to enjoy peaceful use of nuclear energy in accordance with the nuclear Non-Proliferation Treaty.

b. In their view the Additional Protocol is in no way intended to undermine the sovereignty, national dignity or national security of its State Parties.

c. In their view full implementation of Iran's decisions, confirmed by the IAEA's Director General, should enable the immediate situation to be resolved by the IAEA Board.

d. The three governments believe that this will open the way to a dialogue on a basis for longer term co-operation which will provide all parties with satisfactory assurances relating to Iran's nuclear power generation programme. Once international concerns, including those of the three governments, are fully resolved Iran could expect easier access to modern technology and supplies in a range of areas.

e. They will co-operate with Iran to promote security and stability in the region including the establishment of a zone free from weapons of mass destruction in the Middle East in accordance with the objectives of the United Nations.

Source: 'Statement by the Iranian Government and visiting EU foreign ministers', Tehran, 21 Oct. 2003, URL <http://www.iaea.org/NewsCenter/Focus/Iaea Iran/statement_iran21102003.shtml>.

The EU–Iran agreement of 15 November 2004 (the Paris Agreement)

The Government of the Islamic Republic of Iran and the Governments of France, Germany and the United Kingdom, with the support of the High Representative of the European Union (E3/EU), reaffirm the commitments in the Tehran Agreed Statement of 21 October 2003 and have decided to move forward, building on that agreement.

The E3/EU and Iran reaffirm their commitment to the NPT.

The E3/EU recognise Iran's rights under the NPT exercised in conformity with its obligations under the Treaty, without discrimination.

Iran reaffirms that, in accordance with Article II of the NPT, it does not and will not seek to acquire nuclear weapons. It commits itself to full cooperation and transparency with the IAEA. Iran will continue implementing voluntarily the Additional Protocol pending ratification.

To build further confidence, Iran has decided, on a voluntary basis, to continue and extend its suspension to include all enrichment related and reprocessing activities, and specifically: the manufacture and import of gas centrifuges and their components; the assembly, installation, testing or operation of gas centrifuges; work to undertake any plutonium separation, or to construct or operate any plutonium separation installation; and all tests or production at any uranium conversion installation. The IAEA will be notified of this suspension and invited to verify and monitor it. The suspension will be implemented in time for the IAEA to confirm before the November Board that it has been put into effect. The suspension will be sustained while negotiations proceed on a mutually acceptable agreement on long-term arrangements.

The E3/EU recognize that this suspension is a voluntary confidence building measure and not a legal obligation.

Sustaining the suspension, while negotiations on a long-term agreement are under way, will be essential for the continuation of the overall process. In the context of this suspension, the E3/EU and Iran have agreed to begin negotiations, with a view to reaching a mutually acceptable agreement on long term arrangements. The agreement will provide objective guarantees that Iran's nuclear programme is exclusively for peaceful purposes. It will equally provide firm guarantees on nuclear, technological and economic cooperation and firm commitments on security issues.

A steering committee will meet to

launch these negotiations in the first half of December 2004 and will set up working groups on political and security issues, technology and cooperation, and nuclear issues. The steering committee shall meet again within three months to receive progress reports from the working groups and to move ahead with projects and/or measures that can be implemented in advance of an overall agreement.

In the context of the present agreement and noting the progress that has been made in resolving outstanding issues, the E3/EU will henceforth support the Director General reporting to the IAEA Board as he considers appropriate in the framework of the implementation of Iran's Safeguards Agreement and Additional Protocol.

The E3/EU will support the IAEA Director General inviting Iran to join the Expert Group on Multilateral Approaches to the Nuclear Fuel Cycle.

Once suspension has been verified, the negotiations with the EU on a Trade and Cooperation Agreement will resume. The E3/EU will actively support the opening of Iranian accession negotiations at the WTO.

Irrespective of progress on the nuclear issue, the E3/EU and Iran confirm their determination to combat terrorism, including the activities of Al Qa'ida and other terrorist groups such as the MeK. They also confirm their continued support for the political process in Iraq aimed at establishing a constitutionally elected Government.

the agreement signed in Paris on 15 November 2004', IAEA document INFCIRC/637, 26 Nov. 2004, URL <http: // www. iaea. org / Publications/ Documents/ Infcircs / 2004 / infcirc637. pdf>.

Source: IAEA, 'Communication dated 26 November 2004 received from the permanent representatives of France, Germany, the Islamic Republic of Iran and the United Kingdom concerning

Appendix B. The EU non-proliferation clause

Countering proliferation of weapons of mass destruction

The Parties consider that the proliferation of weapons of mass destruction and their means of delivery, both to state and non-state actors, represents one of the most serious threats to international stability and security. The Parties therefore agree to co-operate and to contribute to countering the proliferation of weapons of mass destruction and their means of delivery through full compliance with and national implementation of their existing obligations under international disarmament and non-proliferation treaties and agreements and other relevant international obligations. The parties agree that this provision constitutes an essential element of this agreement.

The parties furthermore agree to cooperate and to contribute to countering the proliferation of weapons of mass destruction and their means of delivery by:

– taking steps to sign, ratify, or accede to, as appropriate, and fully implement all other relevant international instruments;
– the establishment of an effective system of national export controls, controlling the export as well as transit WMD related of goods [*sic*], including a WMD end-use control on dual use technologies and containing effective sanctions for breaches of export controls.*

The Parties agree to establish a regular political dialogue that will accompany and consolidate these elements.

———

Source: European Union, Council, 'Note from the General Secretariat', 19 Nov. 2003, 14997/03 PESC 690, CODUN 45, CONOP 54. COARM 16+COPR 1, attachment to annex 1, available on the SIPRI website at URL <http://www.sipri.org/contents/expcon/wmd_mainstreaming.pdf>.

---

* These two elements might be considered as essential elements on a case by case basis.

About the authors

Christer Ahlström, PhD (Sweden) has been deputy director of SIPRI since August 2002. Previously, he served as a deputy director in the Swedish Ministry for Foreign Affairs on issues related to disarmament and non-proliferation of weapons of mass destruction. He contributed to the SIPRI Yearbook in 2003 and 2004 on the issues of ballistic missile non-proliferation and withdrawal from arms control treaties, respectively.

Heidar Ali Balouji (Iran) is the resident representative in Stockholm, Sweden, of the Institute for Political and International Studies (IPIS), Tehran. He has worked for 10 years on disarmament and international security issues and has published several articles, the most recent being 'Iran's approach towards a nuclear option', *Yaderny Control*, summer 2003, and [Can a war on proliferation be legitimate? The case of Iraq], *Mahnameh Ettelaat Syasi & Eghtesadi* [Monthly on Political and Economic Information], in Oct. 2004 (in Farsi). He has finalized his PhD thesis on the WMD regimes and Iran's national security.

Rory Keane, PhD (Ireland) is a senior researcher with the International Security and Information Service (ISIS) Europe, Brussels, and a part-time consultant with the United Nations Institute for Disarmament Research (UNIDIR). His most recent publications include 'European security and defence policy: from Cologne to Sarajevo', *Global Society*, vol. 19, no. 1 (Jan. 2005); 'The partnership–conditionality binary in the Western Balkans: Promoting local ownership for sustainable democratic transition', *Cambridge Review of International Affairs*, vol. 18, no. 1 (July 2005); and 'European security and defence policy: From Cologne to Sarajevo', *Global Society*, vol. 19, no. 1 (Jan. 2005). He is an expert on post-conflict peace-building and has followed Iranian politics for a number of years. His PhD is from the University of Limerick, Ireland.

Shannon N. Kile (USA) is a researcher on the SIPRI Non-proliferation and Export Controls Project, focusing on nuclear arms control and non-proliferation issues. He has contributed to numerous SIPRI publications, including chapters on nuclear arms control and non-proliferation for the SIPRI Yearbook since 1995. His recent work has concentrated on nuclear proliferation issues related to Iran and North Korea, where he has travelled regularly.

Gerrard Quille, PhD (UK) is a specialist on security and defence policy in the Policy Department of the European Parliament. At the time of writing he was director of the Programme on Non-Proliferation, Arms Control and Disarmament at ISIS Europe. He has published extensively on the EU's evolving security policy and in particular on the European Security Strategy and the European Security and Defence Policy (ESDP).

Jalil Roshandel, PhD (Iran) is a visiting professor in political science at Duke University, North Carolina, USA. He received his PhD in political science from the Université des Sciences Sociales in Toulouse, France, in 1989, followed by a Certificate of Achievement in Peace Research from the International University of Oslo, Norway, in 1989. He has held research and teaching positions at several institutions, including the University of Tehran and the IPIS in Iran, the Copenhagen Peace Research Institute (COPRI) in Denmark, the Middle East Technical University in Turkey, the Stanford University Centre for International Security and Cooperation (CISAC), USA, and most recently the University of California, Los Angeles (UCLA), USA.

Seyed Kazem Sajjadpour (Iran) is a former general director of the IPIS in Tehran and currently a senior fellow there.

Index